PEOPLE IN THE JESUS STORY

James Martin

THE SAINT ANDREW PRESS
EDINBURGH

First published in 1980 by
THE SAINT ANDREW PRESS
121 George Street, Edinburgh EH2 4YN

Copyright © James Martin, 1980

ISBN 0 7152 0436 X

Printed and bound in Great Britain by
Bell and Bain Ltd., Glasgow

PEOPLE IN THE
JESUS STORY

Contents

Preface

To my mind there is no story in all the world either so important or so gripping as that story of Jesus preserved in the four small books that we call 'gospels'. In that story certain characters emerge large and strong. This little book is no more than an attempt to bring some of these characters into the centre of the stage for the reader. My hope is that in so doing I may share with him something of the fascination and even the inspiration they have afforded to me. The characters selected are taken from the three major acts in the drama of Jesus: his birth, his suffering and death, his resurrection.

PART I.
People in the Christmas Story

The Shepherds
(Luke 2: 8–16)

If you go to Bethlehem today you will find it a considerably larger place than the 'little town' of New Testament times. Nowadays it has a population of some forty thousand inhabitants, all of them Arabs and most of these Roman Catholic Christians. But adjacent to the town, and probably not a great deal different in general appearance from what it was in those New Testament times, is what is known as the Field of the Shepherds.

This consists of a string of fields lying in the valley. From very early times these fields have been identified as the region where 'shepherds watched their flocks by night'. Close by is a village which is to this day known as 'The Village of the Watching'. It was here, in the time of Jesus, that shepherds gathered their sheep together at close of day so as to secure them into one large flock for the hours of darkness. This enabled them to take it in turns to watch over the sheep and also take it in turns to eat and to rest.

In the morning the individual flocks were easily separated from one another. Each shepherd simply stood and called his sheep to him. The sheep all knew their own shepherd's voice and responded at once; so that very quickly they were all on their way to the pastures for the day, as they had been arranged round the camp fire the previous evening.

It was to a group of shepherds in the 'night-flocking' area outside Bethlehem – The Shepherd's Field – that there came the first news of the birth of that very special baby who was to become the Saviour of the World.

We could do a great deal worse than think about these shepherds for a while. It is worth reflecting, for a start, that the shepherds to whom came the first news of the first Christmas were just ordinary people who were going about their daily business just in their usual sort of way. That is to say, the first Christmas tidings of great joy were not given to special people engaged on some kind of special task. The marvellous news that was to change the world's history was given first to a group of average men performing a run-of-the-mill job.

Whatever else this may mean, it surely means that Christmas, and all it stands for, is not just for special people. It is for the ordinary people too, living ordinary, routine kind of lives. We should thank God for that. It is indisputable that the vast majority of us are ordinary men and women. Abraham Lincoln once said, 'God must have loved ordinary people very much. He made so many of them.'

The shepherds of the Christmas story are a vivid reminder that Christmas and the Christmas saviour are not just for outstanding individuals like the wise men, but are for the average man and woman too. They are for ordinary people with the usual sorts of joys and sorrows, hopes and fears, sins and temptations.

The wonderful basic truth behind this is that God's love has no favourites. As Augustine once put it, 'He loves us all as if there were only one of us to love.' 'Love came down at Christmas', and that love is big enough to include you and me just as much as any other person of whom we can think.

In that perhaps greatest of all Bible texts, *John* 3: 16, 'God so loved the world that he gave his only Son, that whoever believes in him should not perish but have eternal life', the 'whoever' stands for every single person in the world. That text can be made to read, with complete and dependable truth, 'God so loved the world that he gave his only Son, that James Martin, through believing in him, should not perish, but have eternal life.' And anyone's name can be made to stand there if he or she chooses, for the shepherds make it plain that all are included.

To the shepherds in the flat area round Bethlehem came the news of the saviour's birth, and the vision that this event was for their benefit and for the benefit of all mankind. Simultaneously they were afforded a great opportunity, the opportunity to go and see the infant saviour. Some of them at least took the opportunity, went up to the nearby town, found the baby lying in his manger cradle and knelt before him in homage.

The narrative does not say, but we may safely take it that not all of the shepherds made the short journey to Bethlehem and to the new born King. The intimation and the invitation were given equally to all of them, but not all responded. Some would not believe, some would not be bothered, some were just afraid that there might be awkward or even dangerous repercussions if they went to see the baby.

At any rate, many of the shepherds, for one reason or another, did not go in search of Jesus. But some of them did go and it changed their lives. It did not make any of them suddenly rich and it did not afford to any of them an instant solution to his problems. It did not lead to an easier passage through life, with all the difficulties and the trials and the sorrows removed from the path. It did not even lead to an easier job for any of them.

After they had found and paid homage to the infant Jesus, they had to return to their sheep-watching. Their lives contained as many problems and difficulties as ever before. There were still as many potential sources of anxiety and sorrow. The circumstances of their lives were really much the same despite the fact they had heard this wonderful news and seen this wonderful child.

But *they* were now different. They still had to face the same old things that everybody else had to face in some degree; but they were able to face these things in a different fashion now, because of the fact that they had looked on the face of Jesus.

When a man meets with the Christ child and puts his hand in his, that does not release him from the troubles of this life. Commitment to Jesus does not do away with the stresses and the trials and the obligations of our daily lives. To have met with Jesus, however, can mean for us, as it did for the shepherds, that we acquire a changed attitude to all such things. For now we may know that, with his friendship to support and to hold us, there is nothing, either in life or in death, that need finally defeat us.

Despite having met with Jesus, we will still have our daily work to go through, but we will be able to attend to it all the more happily. We will still have our problems to grapple with, but we will be able to face them all the more patiently. We will still have our sorrows to endure, but we will be able to bear them more courageously. We will still have all the usual storms of human life to face, but we will be able to face them with more resolution. We will still some day have to die, but because we are Christ's and he is ours we will gain the victory even here.

> I've found a Friend: O, such a Friend,
> So kind, and true, and tender!
> So wise a Counsellor and Guide,
> So mighty a Defender!
> From Him who loves me now so well
> What power my soul shall sever?
> Shall life or death, shall earth or hell?
> No! I am his for ever.

The shepherds, inevitably, because of their marvellous experience and the new attitude it gave them to all the circumstances that might attend them, found that life presented a new challenge. They acquired a whole fresh outlook on the business of living.

How could it have been any other way? How could they possibly have returned from the manger and resumed living in just the same fashion as before? How could they possibly have been content to be just the same kind of people as they had been, now that they knew the world's saviour was so close at hand?

And how can we? For the child born at Bethlehem to save the world, including us, is very close at hand. He is in fact much nearer to us than he was to the shepherds on Bethlehem's plains. Now, crucified and risen, he is 'closer to us than breathing, nearer than hands and feet.'

The Wise Men
(*Matthew* 2: 1–11)

Perhaps the most colourful characters in the Christmas story, certainly those that are most likely to stir the imagination, are those usually referred to as the 'wise men'. In fact, however, while we often think of them as belonging to the Christmas Eve/Christmas Day period, they really came upon the scene at a later stage. That is why, in its calendar of the Christian year, the church commemorates the wise men not on Christmas Day but on Epiphany.

The day set aside for special remembrance of the wise men comes not at the beginning of the Christmas season but at the end, not the first day of Christmas but the twelfth. This circumstance derives from the fact that the visit of the wise men to the infant Jesus did not take place on Christmas Day, as is often assumed, but somewhat later, perhaps days, perhaps weeks, perhaps even months. It may be significant that the narrative (*Matthew* 2: 11) speaks of them 'entering the *house*' to see the child with Mary his mother. It may be significant, too, that when Herod ordered the massacre of children in Bethlehem and its neighbourhood, it was the children up to two years of age whose murder he commanded.

It is certainly of significance that their journey must have taken the wise men a very long time. At any rate there is no doubt that they did not reach Jesus until some time after the first Christmas Day. Let me now ask, and try to answer, three questions concerning these wise men.

Who were they? This is not a question that can be

answered with any exactness or with any great degree of assurance, except to say that they came from distant parts and that they were men of much knowledge and great learning.

These men, who are most commonly – and most affectionately – known as the 'wise men', are more properly referred to as the Magi. This is the Greek word by which they are described in the gospel narrative. It is not easy to translate which is the very reason that we are probably just as well to call them Magi, as many scholars do.

They were philosophers and scientists – and astrologers as well. The *New English Bible*, indeed, translates Magi as 'astrologers'. One of the academic interests of these men, who belonged to the intelligentsia of the age, was the study of the stars and their meaning. This was what drew them from their homes and across many hundreds of miles to the cradle of Jesus.

Legend has it that the wise men were kings and has even given them names – Melchior, Caspar and Balthazar. Their royal blood and their names are given musical proclamation in the very popular carol 'We Three Kings of Orient Are'. It may well be that the wise men were in fact kings. There is no doubt that they were men of much wealth. To be able to engage in such studies as they did, to be able to make such a long journey as was involved in following the Christmas star, and to be able to bring such costly presents as they carried, these things indicate that they were men of very considerable means.

The New Testament nowhere tells us just how many wise men there were. Some legends say there were twelve of them, but, in the main, legend is agreed that there were three. This is probably correct. At any rate, the fact that three gifts are mentioned suggests very strongly that there were three men to bring them.

We cannot give a very explicit answer to the question,

'Who were the wise men?', but we can reasonably assume that they were three in number and that they came from distant Gentile lands. One at least may have been a coloured man, but at any rate they seem to have come from different countries and from far away.

For that reason the wise men symbolise vividly that the Christian gospel is for every man, irrespective of his race, colour, circumstances or position. Jesus Christ came to this earth for all men, died for all men, was raised from the dead for all men, and lives for all men. Jesus was born to offer himself as saviour for every single man, woman and child in the world. Salvation was bought at a great cost but it is free for each and all to accept and share. That is part of the message that is enshrined in the wise men and their journey to the infant Jesus.

Jesus was born a Jew, into a Jewish home and into a Jewish village, and the first who acclaimed him were men of his own race, shepherds from the nearby plain. But the others who came shortly after with their homage – foreigners from distant lands – symbolise that Jesus came not to be saviour of the Jews only but also of the Gentiles, not just of some people, but of all.

The child of Bethlehem came to be saviour of all men, of man of every race and of every land and of every colour. What is more, he came for the benefit of every *kind* of man, not just for certain classes or certain types but for all. He came to save the sinner, to rescue the lost, to give help to the needy, to strengthen the weak, to comfort the sad, to give hope to the dying.

This means that Jesus loves and wants all the people that we know, not just the likeable ones but the unpleasant ones as well. The love of God came down to earth in Jesus for all men, including the tough guys and the rascals, those who have terrible tongues, those who take too much alcoholic liquor, those who have awful morals, even those we simply cannot abide.

And do you recall that in order to come to Jesus's side, the wise men had to crouch down very low and practically crawl through the very low entrance to the stable? That at least, is how tradition has pictured it; and if you should go to Bethlehem today and visit the Church of the Nativity, built over the birthplace of Jesus, you will find that the way in is through a door so low that you cannot enter unless you are prepared to bend down. There is surely an analogy here of the need to be humble in approaching Jesus.

The second question is, *What was involved in this journey that the wise men made to find and pay homage to Jesus?*

The activity of their minds was involved in the making of this journey. These men were the thinkers of the age, the intellectuals, the leaders of thought. Yet they counted it worth while, a necessity even, that they should follow the leading of the star.

It is not an uncommon idea today that, if a man is to follow Christ, he must leave his thinking faculties behind. Many people have the opinion that Christian belief and honest thought cannot be companions. This, however, is utter nonsense; and the wise men are a reminder that Jesus asks for the worship and the service of our minds as well as of our hearts and our wills.

The facing of dangers and the enduring of hardships were also involved in that journey. In those days it was an extremely hazardous undertaking to travel as far as they did. Roads were little more than tracks and paths in many parts. Brigands were numerous and practised their trade with zeal, cunning and often ferocity. Wild animals were a constant threat.

Despite all the perils and difficulties that were an inevitable accompaniment of an expedition such as they undertook, the wise men counted it well worth while simply for the satisfaction of following the star and of finding their way to the new-born King.

In this is symbolised the challenge of Christ to the brave and the adventurous within us. Jesus calls us to no easy way but to one that asks for the best that we have and the utmost we can give.

It proved worth while for the wise men who followed the star and it will always prove worth while for anyone who follows Christ today. The risk of hardship and the possibility of sacrifice are inevitably present but this is the road that leads to life at its best.

The third question is *Why did they make the journey? What was its purpose?*

It was to find their way to the new-born King. The aim of the wise men was to find their way to Jesus. They achieved that aim, of course. The road was long and difficult; it was perilous and exacting. But eventually they reached journey's end. When they did, they gave Jesus their homage and they presented to him their gifts. The consequence was that they themselves went away enriched.

Here, too, the wise men serve as a symbol. They symbolise that Jesus expects that all who make their way to his feet will pay him their homage and present to him their gifts. He asks for their trust and their commitment. The wise men brought expensive gifts to Jesus. But, then, they were wealthy people. Jesus neither expects nor wants the same gifts from all. Some people's gifts will necessarily be less lavish than those of others, but may be equally valuable to Jesus all the same. We may give only what we have and what we are. When we do give to Jesus whatever we have to give, we ourselves are at the same time and by the same action made rich.

> What can I give him?
> Poor as I am?
> If I were a shepherd,
> I would bring a lamb;
> If I were a wise man,
> I would do my part;

> Yet what I can I give him
> Give my heart.

At the same time, it is worth looking in some detail at the actual gifts which the wise men brought to Jesus for each gift was appropriate for the occasion.

First there was *gold*, and gold has always been the royal metal, the gift fitted for a king. This was a symbol of Jesus's 'royal degree'. For he *was* a king. Even lying there in the straw in all his infant weakness, he was still a king, the King of Kings.

Undoubtedly Jesus came into this world in order to reign. He did not come, it is true, to reign in the way that the bulk of his countrymen were expecting Messiah to come and reign. His purpose was not to rule by force over men's temporal affairs, but to rule by love over men's hearts.

This means that, since Jesus is our King, he ought to have our unqualified allegiance. He demands our utmost loyalty, a loyalty that will compel us to acknowledge him and to honour him wherever we find ourselves, not just on Sundays and not just in church, but always and everywhere, so that it will be obvious to all who meet us whose we are and whom we serve.

John Buchan tells the story of how one of Prince Charlie's followers was put under threat of death after the Battle of Culloden Moor. With drawn sword his enemy said to him, 'Renounce Charles or die.' To which the defiant highlander, with death at his very elbow, replied, 'You may take my head from my body, but you will never take my heart from my king.'

That is the kind of loyalty that King Jesus hopes to have from every one of us.

The second gift was *frankincense* and this was an equally fitting gift for it was the symbol of deity. This incense was burned in the temple as an offering to God and here it was appropriately given to the infant Jesus, for although

> A little child the Saviour came,
> The mighty God was still his name.

The baby of Bethlehem was none other than the very
'Word made flesh'. In him we see God face to face and
can get to know God's very nature. The child born to
Mary on the first Christmas Day was altogether man
and altogether God. This is the wonder of the
incarnation. Jesus was not half man and half God. That
would have been simply a poor hybrid creature who
was really nothing at all, neither one thing nor the
other.

Jesus, however, was both man and God, at one and
the same time fully human and fully divine. This is
something which our minds cannot properly comprehend.
We must only accept it and marvel at it; and it is of this
that the gift of frankincense speaks.

Some scholars suggest that frankincense is best taken
in this context as the symbol of Jesus's priesthood. It
was in the worship of the Temple that the sweet
perfume of frankincense was used and the suggestion is
that it is best thought of here as speaking of Jesus as
priest.

It is true that in a real and very wonderful fashion
Jesus was our priest, the priest being one who created a
contact between God and the worshipper. The Latin for
priest is *pontifex*, a word which literally means 'bridge-
builder'. Jesus certainly was that. He built a bridge
between man and God. Indeed he himself is the bridge
that makes it possible for anyone at all to cross over
into the very presence of God.

The third gift of the wise men was *myrrh*. This also
was a fitting gift to bring to Jesus, for this was what was
used to embalm a dead body. The gift of myrrh was a
reminder, therefore, that Jesus's mission of winning
salvation for the world could be accomplished only at

the cost of his life. Even in the manger of Bethlehem, the cross of Calvary was already present.

One of Holman Hunt's paintings represents this truth. Entitled 'The Shadow of the Cross', it shows Jesus coming to the door of the carpenter's shop in Nazareth. It is near the closing of the day and, as the tired Jesus stretches out his arms above his head, the rays of the setting sun cast on the wall behind him a shadow in the shape of a cross.

The picture is an indication that from the beginning the end was inevitable and the gift of myrrh symbolises the same truth, Christmas and Easter being very close together. The baby born on Christmas Day had to die on the cross in order to bring us eternal life.

We three kings of Orient are:
Bearing gifts we traverse afar.
Field and fountain, moor and mountain
Following yonder star.

Melchior:
Born a King on Bethlehem's plain
Gold I bring, to crown him again –
King for ever, ceasing never,
Over us all to reign.

Caspar:
Frankincense to offer have I:
Incense owns a deity nigh:
Prayer and praising, all men raising,
Worship him, God most high.

Balthazar:
Myrrh is mine; its bitter perfume
Breathes a life of gathering gloom;
Sorrowing, sighing, bleeding, dying,
Sealed in the stone-cold tomb.

Glorious now, behold him arise,
King, and God, and Sacrifice!
Heaven sings alleluya,
Alleluya, the earth replies.

The Innkeeper
(*Luke* 2: 7)

There can be few more poignantly haunting sentences in the whole range of English literature than this simple sentence of the Bible in the *King James's Version*: 'There was no room for them in the inn.' Nor can there be many more tragic figures than the innkeeper who failed to find room in his establishment for the birth of history's most important baby.

The innkeeper presents a figure that is not only universally acknowledged as tragic, but also universally regarded with something approaching shocked horror. How could anyone behave as he did, turning away from his door the woman who was on the very point of giving birth to the saviour of the world?

I wonder if we have ever stopped to reflect that this innkeeper was in all likelihood quite a decent fellow, no worse, if no better, than others in his line of business. The chances are that the reasons behind his refusal to find space in his inn for Mary and her coming child not only seemed perfectly good and valid reasons to him but would have seemed just as good and sound to anyone else in the same circumstances. It is, in fact, extremely likely that we ourselves, placed in the same situation as he, would have come to exactly the same conclusion and on the same grounds.

Let us try to put ourselves in his place if we can. Here he was, summoned to the door very late at night after an exceedingly long and exhausting day. The Roman authorities had ordered a census to be taken of all the inhabitants of Palestine, with each family having to register in the ancestral town of its male head. One consequence of this was that there was a great influx of visitors to Bethlehem in order to comply with the census requirement.

All day the crowds had been pouring in to the 'little town', seeking temporary lodgings. Many had found accommodation with relatives or friends. Quite a large number, too, had come to the inn for shelter. The innkeeper had been on his feet practically all day and far into the evening, squeezing guests into every available corner.

And now two extremely late stragglers appeared at his door in search of a room. True, the woman was obviously in a very advanced stage of pregnancy and was plainly in a very exhausted state. But there was nothing else he could do but turn them away.

For one thing, he was much too busy to take on any more. He had been hard at it all day and simply could not cope with anything else.

For a second thing, his inn was already bursting at the seams. It was full to capacity and a bit more, if the truth be told. As a matter of fact it had been choc-a-bloc for hours, and already he had had to turn away other hopeful enquirers.

For another thing, he could not even attempt to meet their needs without almost certain financial cost to himself and, after all, he had his living to make. That is why he was in business, wasn't he? Quite plainly he could squeeze in this couple only by expelling others or by restricting the accommodation already assigned to them. No, nothing could be done for them. That was beyond doubt. His bread and butter must come first. Anyone would agree to that. He could not afford to lose money for some mere sentimental whim and that is what it would come to if he decided to swing open his door for these two latecomers to enter. Anyone could see at a glance that they were poor. He could hope for no cash recompense from them for taking pity on them, but he could certainly count on losing the goodwill of the customers he inconvenienced.

No, it just could not be done. No one could say that he was a hard man. He was as kind and as compassionate as the next man, and he would genuinely have liked to help. But it was out of the question and he would be the worst kind of fool to try. He simply had not the time; there was no room; and it would be much too costly.

The innkeeper was right, of course. He *would* have been a fool to take the strangers in under the prevailing circumstances. From every human standpoint he was right. Yet how bitterly he must have regretted his action when in later years he discovered who it was he had turned away, when he found out that he had refused the best chance of his life.

I suggested that we try to put ourselves in the innkeeper's place. I want to ask now if perhaps we really are in his place. Are we perhaps refusing to let Jesus have room in our lives and for the very reasons that influenced the innkeeper?

Perhaps we are too busy. We would like to take our religion seriously, so we persuade ourselves. We really wish we could let Jesus be our complete Lord and Master. But we just cannot find time for that. We have too many other things to see to, things that simply must be given our attention.

Perhaps we have no room. If Jesus is let in to a human life, certain other things have to go, things like selfishness and dishonesty and bad temper, and a great many more. There simply is not room for them and for Jesus as well; and it may be that we are reluctant to have these other things disturbed.

Perhaps we fear that to let Jesus into our lives would hinder us from getting on in the world and from making so much money as we would like to do – and of course material comfort must come first.

The fact is that the innkeeper was not an oddity, a human freak. In every age – including our own – the world contains a great many decent, good-living, well-intentioned people who would like, if circumstances were different, to admit Jesus to their lives in a full-blown sense. But with things the way they are, they conclude that they just cannot do it and that they would be foolish to try.

They are quite right, of course. They would be foolish to let Jesus in. But what an opportunity they are missing and how much they may regret passing it by.

> If love should count you worthy and should deign
> One day to seek your door and be your guest,
> Pause! ere you draw the bolt and bid Him rest,
> If in your old content you would remain.
> For not alone He enters: in his train
> Are angels of the mists, the lonely quest,
> Dreams of the unfulfilled and unpossessed,
> And sorrow, and life's immemorial pain.
>
> He wakes desires you never may forget,
> He shows you stars you never saw before,
> He makes you share with him, for evermore,
> The burden of the world's divine regret.
> How wise you were to open not – and yet
> How poor if you should turn Him from the door.

> (S.R. Lysaght, 'The Penalty of Love')

These lines express rather well what was at stake for the innkeeper on the first Christmas Eve, just as they put their fingers on the issues involved today in a man's confrontation with the baby born at Bethlehem. To let Jesus into our lives is to admit disturbance and cost and probably sacrifice. But it is also to welcome the richest and fullest kind of living it is possible to know, so rich and full that none of life's ills will be able to spoil it and not even death will bring it to an end.

The innkeeper, of course, was in no position to be aware of the implications of his decision to say 'no' to

Mary and Joseph. How could he have known then the
importance of the unborn child he was turning away? If
he had known, what a difference that knowledge would
surely have made that first Christmas Eve. Here are a
few lines from a poem that pursues this line of thought.
The poem is entitled 'The Landlord speaks':

> ...Could I know
> That they were so important? Just the two,
> No servants, just a workman sort of man,
> Leading a donkey, and his wife thereon,
> Drooping and pale...
> There was a sign, they say, a heavenly light
> Resplendent; but I had no time for stars.
> And there were songs of angels in the air
> Out on the hills; but how was I to hear
> Amid the thousand clamours of an inn?
> Of course, if I had known them, who they were,
> And who he that should be born that night –
> ...Had I known,
> I would have turned the whole inn upside down,
> ...Alas! Alas! To miss a chance like that!
> This inn that might be chief among them all,
> The birthplace of Messiah – had I known.

The innkeeper makes a tragic figure, indeed. But,
then, he was not aware of who it was he was turning
away. Many turn away Jesus in full awareness of who
he is. Their tragedy is all the more awful.

Herod the Great
(*Matthew* 2: 1–18)

One who looms large in the Christmas story but who himself never set eyes on Jesus is Herod the Great.

Herod was a powerful ruler and held the reins of government in his strong hands for many years. Having shown himself to be both a dependable collaborator and also an efficient administrator, he was appointed by the Romans to rule over Palestine, first as governor in 47 BC and then as king in 40 BC. He remained on the throne until he died in 4 BC.

In Matthew's gospel we encounter Herod as a cruel and ruthless despot who was prepared to murder innocent children in an attempt to eliminate a vague threat to his kingship. This side of his nature was no doubt always present, although in his younger years he could be very magnanimous, but the fear and suspicion which could produce such savage disregard for human life had grown in strength as he had grown in age. The older he got the more Herod seemed to be looking over his shoulder for possible threats to his position.

Many people lost their lives simply because Herod thought they were about to pose a threat to him. The consequence was that he was prepared even to commit murder amongst his own family as protection against fancied danger. His wife, Mariamne, her mother, Alexandra, and three of his own sons were amongst those who were put to death at his command. His savagery became a legend in his own lifetime so that in a now famous saying his friend Augustus, Emperor of Rome, once remarked, 'It is safer to be Herod's pig than his son.'

This cruel side of Herod's nature was given a somewhat morbid illustration when, in his seventies, he went to live in the beautifully lush city of Jericho. Realising that the end of his life could not be far distant, he had a number of Jerusalem's best known citizens arrested and held in custody. His orders were that, as soon as he died, they were all to be executed. Well aware of his unpopularity, and knowing only too well that no one would mourn his passing, he was determined, he said, to ensure that some would shed tears for his death.

Herod had other qualities. He was a strong and, in the main, competent ruler. Rome would not have permitted him to continue so long in a position of such authority unless he had proved satisfactory.

Herod is particularly remembered also for the fact that he was a quite indefatigable builder. To this day, if you visit the Holy Land, you will be able to see many memorials to his seemingly inexhaustible industry in this field. Possibly the best known today – and undoubtedly the most dramatic – is the fortress he constructed at Masada on the shores of the Dead Sea.

Herod was not the first to build on the top of Masada, a plateau some half a mile long and one-eighth of a mile broad which towers a striking seventeen hundred feet above the southern end of the Dead Sea. Jonathan Maccabeus was the first to build there but it was Herod the Great who made Masada into the fortress which now stands in the front portals of Jewish history's hall of fame. This is because in 73 AD nearly one thousand beleaguered Jewish nationalists, having resisted a Roman siege for no less than three years, carried out a mass suicide pact rather than fall into the hands of the Roman army that was now on the point of capturing the fortress.

Herod had taken refuge in Masada during a period of crisis in 42 BC when the Parthians captured Jerusalem.

Attracted to the site and alive to its siege-resistant potential, he set to work a few years later and developed Masada in quite astonishing fashion. He made use of virtually the whole of the top of the mountain area to bring into being what was in essence a self-sufficient garrison town, capable of housing comfortably some one thousand people. He built a wall to enclose the whole plateau and inside was placed everything necessary to sustain life – patches of soil for growing crops, water cisterns, storehouses for food and, in addition, a magnificient three-tiered palace erected on the natural terraces at the north end of the cliff.

To create such a fortress town in a location so difficult to reach and in such a barren area was a stupendous feat. Enough of Herod's building remains there to this day to make it plain just how stupendous it was.

While Masada's later history makes it the most romantic of Herod's many building exploits, probably the most significant was his reconstruction of the Temple at Jerusalem. After a great deal of preparatory work, the actual rebuilding commenced in 17 BC and continued for about eighty years. It was still in progress during the lifetime of Jesus and, sadly, was completed only eight years before it was totally destroyed by Titus in the sack of Jerusalem in 70 AD.

Most people, however, remember Herod the Great best for what was surely his most infamous action, the so-called 'massacre of the innocents'. When the Magi, following their guiding star in search of the new-born king, arrived in Jerusalem, Herod came to hear of them and summoned them before him. When he learned of their quest, his obsessive fear of losing his throne once again took over to dominate his thinking and control his actions.

When the Magi chose not to co-operate with him and let him know where this special infant was to be found,

Herod took action himself, in a way that even surpassed any of his previous deeds for merciless savagery. 'In order to locate this one child and kill him', Herod decided, 'I shall kill every child in the area who might conceivably be of the right age. That will make sure that I dispose of the one who is a threat to me.'

So the command was given; and so every child in the neighbourhood under two years of age was put to the sword by Herod's men.

Herod's 'massacre of the innocents' might seem beyond belief if we did not have all too much evidence in much more recent history of the lengths to which men can go in terms of cruelty and denial of basic humanity. The atrocities of war are never very far away and, for instance, horrors such as Hitler's gas-chambers and the like are unforgettable.

But we need not look even so far afield as modern history or current events. We need not even look around at other people and at the cruelties which are inflicted every day by others on young children in our own age and in our own country. We need look no further than ourselves.

How many of us can say with confident honesty that he has never been guilty of doing harm to any child? Before we dare to answer that question in the affirmative we must take account of the fact that harm may be caused to a child not only by what an adult does to him but also, and sometimes even more, by what he fails to do.

One of O. Henry's short stories tells of a man whose wife died while their only daughter was still a child. The father was never actively unkind to the child as he brought her up but he never would take time to play with her or talk to her or listen to her. Whenever she attempted to claim his attention, he would say, 'I'm busy. Go outside and play.' So she took to the streets for her play, and in time she took to the streets for her trade.

When she died and came to the gates of heaven, the story continues, St Peter said to Jesus, 'I've a young woman just arrived who was a bad lot. I suppose I send her straight to hell.' 'No', said Jesus, 'Let her in. But look out for a man who would find no time to spend with his lonely daughter and send *him* to hell.'

The utter inhumanity of Herod's massacre of the innocents stands out starkly in the Christmas scene because it is in such marked contrast to the message of the incarnation. Herod showed not the slightest concern for even the youngest of these innocent children, some of them only babies. Yet in the Jesus whose birth had sparked off Herod's inhuman course of action, the very love of God had come to earth.

> Love is smiling from thy face!
> Strikes for us now the hour of grace,
> Saviour, since thou art born!

One thing more. There is provided for us here an illustration of the truth that, in the long run at least, the power of love is stronger than the power of hate, no matter how much it may seem to the contrary at any given time. More often than not, perhaps, love will appear to be a much weaker force than hate. In this particular instance, even God's love, come to earth in a helpless baby, appeared no match for the malevolence of a powerful earthly monarch.

In fact, of course, that love proved much stronger than Herod's hate. While Herod's little empire soon fell into ruin, the message of God's love come to earth in Jesus swept victoriously across all the world. Love is always stronger than hate in the end, and God's love is the strongest thing in the world.

> Love came down at Christmas,
> Love all lovely, Love Divine:
> Love was born at Christmas,
> Star and angels gave the sign.

Love shall be our token,
Love be yours and love be mine,
Love to God and all men,
Love for plea and gift and sign.

The Child
(*Luke* 2: 11)

It can be very easy, in thinking about the Christmas story, to be so taken up with its subsidiary characters that we almost leave out of account its central character, the child in the manger. And yet he is, of course, the whole reason, properly speaking, for having any Christmas celebrations at all.

Many of us are accustomed to think of Christmas as the 'children's festival', and much of our Christmas celebration has the children right in the middle – the Christmas trees, the parties and the rest. It is perfectly right and proper that this should be so and there is something wonderful about it. But it is nothing short of tragic if we do not remember that Christmas is truly the children's festival only because first and foremost it is the festival of the child, the child born to be our saviour. It is tragic because Christmas without the Christ-child is really not Christmas at all.

I am sure nearly everyone has heard about the woman who was looking through a display of Christmas cards in a shop. Suddenly she came upon one which depicted the nativity and exclaimed in considerable disgust, 'Look at this. They are even bringing religion into Christmas now!'

That may make us laugh but it is supposed to be a true story and the sad fact is that to a great many people Christmas is a time of presents and parties, holiday and entertainments and no more. Now there is nothing wrong with any of the things I have mentioned nor is there anything wrong with having them at Christmas time. In fact there is a lot to be said in their

favour, but they are certainly not the be-all and the end-
all of Christmas and it is a great pity if the basic reason
for making Christmas a bright and happy time should
be forgotten or ignored.

Christmas, you see, is first and foremost a religious
festival. It is the time set apart for remembering the
birth of Jesus.

I remember once speaking to a friend in my own
congregation as Christmas was approaching. 'I don't
like Christmas at all', she said.

I for my part *love* Christmas; and I love most of the
things that go with it. I love the carols and the
Christmas trees, the fairy lights, the tinsel, the holly, the
parties, Santa Claus, the reunions, the giving and
receiving of presents, the special church services. But I
think I know what my friend meant, and I have more
than a little sympathy with her. There are some things
about Christmas, or at least about the way we celebrate
it, that rub me the wrong way, too. I hate, for instance,
the vulgar and ruthless commercial exploitation of
Christmas that seems to increase everywhere year by
year.

There are other things as well which I dislike. One is
the widespread practice of writing 'Xmas' instead of
'Christmas'. What, after all, does *X*mas mean? Is not 'x'
the symbol of anonymity, the mark of someone
unknown or not to be disclosed? And does not this sum
up all that is so often wrong with our celebration of
Christmas? What is desperately needed today is to bring
Christ back into Christmas.

If that were to happen, if Christmas became truly the
festival of the child of Bethlehem, paradoxically the term
'Xmas' might not be so far out after all. For 'x' is, of
course, not only the symbol of anonymity. It is also the
symbol of the cross; and, even as Jesus lay in the
manger on the first Christmas Day, already Calvary was
thrusting its dark shadow across him.

It is very easy to sentimentalise the birth of Jesus. Of course it is a very lovely story; but it is also a sad and terrible one, full of suffering and pain. For love of us and in order to achieve our salvation, the Christ-child had to go to a cross.

One of the many Christmas legends purports to tell how the robin got his red breast. When Jesus was hanging on the cross, so the legend goes, the little robin, anxious to ease the saviour's pain, plucked with her beak a thorn from the mock crown that was tearing Jesus's forehead. As she performed this kindly action, a drop of Jesus's blood fell on her breast and stained it bright red; and ever since, the robin has been red-breasted.

Legend though it is, this story of the origin of the robin's red breast is an illustration of how Christmas and Calvary belong together. I, for one, used to think that the robin redbreast type of Christmas card was quite inappropriate. It seemed to me to have no real relevance to the message of the incarnation. It was when I came across for the first time the legend of how the robin got its red breast that I realised that this kind of Christmas card might not be so unsuitable after all.

Certainly, at any rate, the incarnation and the crucifixion, Christmas and Calvary, are each part of the one story of God's saving love. And to put Christ into Christmas in any personal fashion means putting his cross into our lives.

One Christmas Eve in London there was a snarl-up of traffic which found a large lorry impatiently stuck behind a small private car. In his impatience the lorry driver began to hoot his horn incessantly. At last the driver of the little car could stand it no longer. He wound down his window, stuck out his head and called out, 'Pack it up mate, please. I see you've a bunch of holly in your bonnet. Where you really need the holly is in your heart.'

That is where we all need the Christmas holly – in our hearts! It is so easy, and so common, to have it everywhere else but there, and yet that is where it counts. Sometimes the presence of that holly will prick us and even wound us; but to have it is the only way to make Christmas real.

The child in the manger is far and away the most important character in the Christmas story, and we need to get him back into the centre of Christmas. That means, first of all, making this child of Bethlehem the master of our lives. Who is he, then, this child whose rightful place is at the centre of the Christmas scene? The Bible gives him many names. Here we look at only three, and very briefly.

Long before the first Christmas, the prophet Isaiah foretold the coming of a very special child, who would be known as 'Immanuel'. This is Hebrew for 'God is with us'. This name given long in advance to the child of Bethlehem indicates how in him the very face of God was revealed to mankind.

Through all the ages God had been trying to make himself known to mankind in various ways. Men had responded in varying degrees and had grasped God's self-revelation with varying success. Now God counted the time ripe to enter directly into the human race and so a baby was born in Bethlehem. In him we are able to see for ourselves what God is like and especially to know that his nature is love.

When the baby was actually born, his parents called him 'Jesus'. This name has the same meaning as 'Joshua': 'one who rescues, one who saves'. The name was also given in advance and it is the most fitting of all. For, as the Bible says, Jesus came to save us from our sins.

He came to save us in a double way. First, by obtaining forgiveness for past sins. Human sin was an obstruction between man and God. Jesus came to remove that obstruction, although it was to cost him his life, and to make it possible for anyone who wished it to be forgiven his sins and to enjoy a joyous new relationship with God.

Jesus can rescue a man from his sins in another way, too. He can give him the strength to overcome his temptations and do the right. He can enable him to win free of all those many unworthy things that so often despoil life. He can deliver us from sin and make life for us what God would like it to be.

After Jesus had been crucified and raised from the dead, his followers began to call him 'Lord'. This was the highest title they could find. 'Lord' (in the Greek, *kurios*) was originally a title of respect, something like our 'sir' but it had come to be an equivalent for God. To apply this title to Jesus was for his disciples to acclaim his divinity and at the same time to ascribe to him total sovereignty over their lives.

They began to call him Lord because he had shown himself to be the master of sin and of death; and because they recognised that he sought to be the master of man.

That is the way to make Jesus our saviour – by making him our master. It is when we accord him that position that he is enabled to forgive us our sins and to fashion our lives not only into better but into gladder things, and also to bring us at the last into the sunshine of his heaven.

Simeon and Anna
(*Luke* 2: 21–38)

Sometimes in a great and famous picture there will be a marvellous piece of detail on the edge of the canvas, and sometimes the main theme of the picture will be so beautiful and so moving that the loveliness and the significance of the peripheral detail quite escape us.

The appearance of Simeon and Anna in the Christmas story is a bit like that. They appear on the edge of the canvas, as it were, and many of us may hardly even remember that they figure in the story at all. But they do and, although they are not part of the central action, they are well worth a thought.

After the birth of a baby boy to devout Jewish parents, the religious law required them to do three things. First, they had the child circumcised when he was eight days old. Second, they symbolically bought back their son from God, to whom he really belonged, by paying the sum of five shekels to the priest. This was to be done as soon as possible after the child was thirty-one days old. Third, the mother had to offer a sacrifice for her purification. According to the law the process of childbirth rendered her ceremonially unclean for a period of forty days, and then she had to bring an offering of a lamb, or, if she was poor, two pigeons. The fact that Mary's offering was the alternative one of two pigeons is a clear indication that Jesus was born into a poor family.

Simeon and Anna entered the stage of the Christmas narrative when the holy family came to the Temple in Jerusalem to fulfil the second and third of these religious obligations. The remarkable and important thing they did was to recognise Jesus for the unique child he was. Probably no one else in that crowded Temple area spared a second glance for the peasant couple and their baby. But Simeon and Anna each saw that the baby was special and said so openly. This acknowledgment of the messiahship of the infant Jesus seems to have been ignored by the rest of the Temple visitors that day, but Simeon and Anna for their part were willing, even glad, to testify to the identity they recognised as his.

Neither Simeon nor Anna belonged to the official or professionally religious class; and yet the fact was that they and a few others like them were the real custodians, not to say the saviours, of true religion in the Israel of the day. The priests and the Pharisees and the Scribes were the 'religious' of the period. They were the ones who attended to the ordinances of religion and its obligations. The priests worked at carrying through the various ceremonies and acts of worship that God required to be observed. The Scribes worked at codifying and defining the implications and requirements of the law which God had given to his people. The Pharisees worked at keeping that law's regulations and attempting to ensure that others kept them, too.

These were the people who in the nature of things might have been expected to be closest to God, and therefore most likely to recognise and welcome the Messiah when he came. It did not turn out like that. Somehow they were all so concerned about the letter of God's law that its spirit largely escaped them. They were not – most of them at least – very close to God at all. Had it depended only on them, true religion must have died in the land.

Fortunately it did not depend only on them. There was a small body of people in whom the flame of personal piety was preserved. They had the heart of the matter. They would not have survived one round in a contest of theological debate with any of these others; but they were closer to God than any of them.

This little group of obscure but devout people were called 'The Quiet in the Land'. They spent their lives in prayer and worship; and they genuinely longed for the coming of God's deliverer. Simeon and Anna were of their number; and that is why they were able to recognise the identity of Jesus when his parents brought him to the Temple that day.

It was not those who were theologically and ecclesiastically most knowledgeable who were best prepared to recognise and accept Jesus as Messiah. Most of those in that category proved, in the event, either unable or unwilling to accept him and, indeed, were largely instrumental in engineering his crucifixion. Those who did recognise him were humble folk who could not have claimed any great experience in theological or ecclesiastical matters and did not possess any. They were, however, sincere in their trust in God and in their devotion to his way. That was what gave them the perception to see that the infant Jesus was the promised saviour.

Always it is the heart rather than the head that is the key to visions of God. True devotion matters more than correct doctrine.

This is not to say that doctrine is unimportant. God wants us to pay homage to him with our heads as well as with our hearts. We are to use our minds also to worship and to serve him. But unless our hearts are lovingly given over to him, all the rest loses its value.

There is an old story of the days in Scotland when those aspiring to be counted eligible to receive the communion had to be 'taken through hands', which was to undergo an oral examination in their knowledge of the Bible and of the shorter catechism. An old woman came to her very young minister and expressed her wish

to become a communicant member. The minister
explained what must be done and then proceeded to put
to her a series of questions. The old woman floundered
badly in her answers and eventually the minister said,
'I'm sorry, but you are not yet worthy of the
Communion. Come back again when you have studied
your Bible and your Catechism a bit more.'

His visitor rose to go and her eyes brimmed over with
tears. As she turned away she said, 'I'm sorry I didn't
know the answers to your questions. I just know that I
love the Saviour and I wanted to come to his
Communion.' Cut to the heart the minister cried out,
'Come back. Come back. Here's your token. I see now
that I was wrong. You've got what really matters.'

He was right, and Simeon and Anna confirm that he
was right. They were among the glorious few who gave
a warm welcome to the infant redeemer and it was
because their hearts were in the right place, in tune with
God.

It made all the difference to them, so much so that
they could now await the end of their long lives with a
feeling of mission accomplished and the sense of peace
that goes with it. That is why Simeon could give voice
to that beautiful prayer of impending departure from
this life which, as the *Nunc Dimittis*, has become a
beloved part of the liturgy of many churches. And to
recognise and acclaim Jesus for who he is makes a
mighty difference to anyone and to everyone whatever
stage of life he may have reached.

> Who is he, in yonder stall,
> At whose feet the shepherds fall?
> 'Tis the Lord! O wondrous story.
> 'Tis the Lord, the King of Glory!
> At his feet we humbly fall.
> Crown him, crown him Lord of all!

PART II

People in the Passion Story

Judas Iscariot

The passion of Jesus constitutes the most dramatic event in all history. It is also, as Christians are aware, the most momentous and lies at the very heart of God's plan of salvation. Many arresting figures stride across the stage of this drama. We are going to look at a few of these, seeing them not so much from God's standpoint as from our own, seeing in them something – a great deal perhaps – of ourselves. The first character we take is Judas Iscariot.

The figure of Judas Iscariot is one of the most enigmatic in the whole Bible. Had we been actual observers in those days we could have had no inkling in the beginning as to how things were to turn out. In those happy days when he began his ministry, Jesus called to his side a dozen young men to be his lieutenants in the work. One of those twelve was Judas Iscariot.

The fact that Jesus called Judas in this way and that Judas responded to the call means at least two significant things. It means, for one thing, that Jesus saw in Judas the makings of a real disciple, despite his weaknesses. It means, for another thing, that Judas saw in Jesus a leader so worth following that he left everything to go after him.

This makes the enigma of Judas all the more puzzling. For here was a man for whom Jesus could and would have done so much, a man, moreover, attracted to Jesus and willing, it seemed, to give him the opportunity to work his will in him. Judas was in the company of Jesus from the first. He lived in close fellowship with him for some three years. He was daily, during that time, under the influence of Jesus and exposed to his spell. Despite all this, at the finish he betrayed Jesus to his enemies for a payment of thirty pieces of silver. It seems almost incredible.

Is it so incredible, however? Is this kind of betrayal of Jesus not being repeated frequently in our day in one form or another? It happens again whenever anyone who professes Christ's name plays the traitor to him.

Why did Judas do it? This is the burning question and it has provoked a great deal of thought and produced many theories. Amid all the answers that are suggested one thing comes through loud and clear. The motives that led Judas Iscariot to play the traitor to his master in the terrible fashion he did are often very similar to the motives which lead us to betray that master in our own way.

Greed is one of the answers given and there is little doubt that love of money may have played some part in Judas's treachery. He had already shown himself to possess a mean streak. Was it not he who objected to the waste of money when the expensive ointment was used to anoint Jesus's head? Judas was the one who acted as treasurer for the little disciple band and he appears to have been guilty of pilfering from the common purse. John's gospel is quite blunt about it and calls him 'thief'.

It seems then that, in part at least, Judas played the traitor for what he could get out of it in material terms. Today, still, his followers may sometimes sell Jesus for gain. So far as some professed Christians are concerned, their allegiance to Jesus continues only until and unless their pocket is threatened. All types and classes of people are vulnerable to the threat and to the corruption of materialism.

Avarice is one of the seven deadly sins and many people reckon it the most dangerous of the seven. It is undoubtedly the most enduring. The fires of physical passion, for instance, die down usually with the passing of the years but avarice tends to increase in strength with age.

Jealousy is another suggested motive for Judas's betrayal; and it may well be that this was part of the driving force behind his action. It is certainly a real possibility, one might even say probability, that Judas was jealous of Peter, James and John. They were the inner circle of Jesus's disciples, admitted to a closer intimacy with their leader than the others were permitted to share. The fact that they occupied what might seem to be a favoured position may well have rankled with a man of the stamp of Judas and the rankling may eventually have prompted him to the awful course of action that he took.

There is no question at any rate that jealousy often does lead to Jesus being betrayed by his followers. We need only think of Peter on the shores of Lake Galilee after the resurrection. He has just been given his battle-orders by Jesus when he catches sight of John, the beloved disciple, in the background. Jealousy catches hold of him and he blurts out petulantly, 'What about him? What have you in mind for him?' To which Jesus replies, 'Never mind about him. I have given you your tasks to do. See to them.'

His answer is exactly the same today to any and to all who may feel similar pangs of jealousy. Many of us need that answer at times. When we are inclined to grouse in our hearts about what others are doing or are not doing, when we are resentful that others seem to be getting more prominence or more glory than we for their work for the master, we should listen to Jesus. He is surely saying to us then, 'Get on with *your* work for me. I am depending on you to do it.'

Refusal to accept Christ's claims has also been put forward as the chief reason for Judas's betrayal. Again it

D

may well have been so, at least in part. At first everything was all right and there was no difficulty at all in this regard. But, as Judas began to realise more clearly what was involved, he began to refuse to accept Jesus for who he was and this may well have helped to push him along that road which led eventually to his kiss of betrayal in the Garden of Gethsemane.

In our own day a man's unwillingness to accept Christ's claims for himself make it so much easier for that man to betray him when a crisis comes. And yet Jesus so evidently justifies all the claims he makes.

Some have put forward the suggestion that Judas's betrayal was really an *attempt to force Jesus's hand*. According to this theory Judas was well intentioned but impatient. He was truly on Jesus's side and wanted his cause to prosper; but he thought Jesus was far too slow, even dilatory, in getting to the point. And so Judas hit on a plan that would force his leader into action. He would engineer it so that Jesus fell into the hands of the religious authorities who hated him and were anxious to put a stop to his activities. When this happened Jesus would have no alternative except to use his powers in a way that he had never used them before and bring in his kingdom not someday or gradually, but now.

Even if this is the true reading of the situation, and Judas did genuinely hope to further Jesus's cause by the action that he took, the inescapable fact remains that it was still an act of treachery. For it meant that he did not have sufficient confidence in Jesus. He thought that he knew better than Jesus did. He reckoned that his way was superior to Jesus's way. On that score what he did was as much an act of treachery as if he were deliberately seeking only harm for Jesus.

Today this kind of treachery still takes place in many places and in many ways. Sometimes we ourselves may be guilty of it. It happens every time we insist on going our own way at the expense of Jesus's way. The fact is that our way is never as good as his way. Judas found that out and so shall we.

Revenge is yet another thing that has been suggested as the chief reason behind the course of action adopted by Judas Iscariot. Some think that what he did was by way of being retaliation for bitter disappointment.

Judas, it is suggested, came into Jesus's service with high hopes that substantial material benefits would accrue to him as a result of that service. Gradually the realisation came home to him more and more forcibly that he had misread the situation. The kingdom Jesus had come to inaugurate was not a material but a spiritual one. Jesus had come to establish himself not as king of any country or nation but as king of the hearts of men.

As this realisation dawned, Judas felt let down. As this feeling intensified, Judas began to be enraged and was seized with the desire to hit back and inflict some hurt on Jesus in return for the hurt which he himself had sustained.

It happens still in our day that men come to Jesus's side with false hopes. They confidently expect him to lead them into material prosperity and to keep them free from hardship and from pain. In fact, however, Jesus never promised such rewards to his followers. The rewards he promises are of a different nature – things like victory over life's adversities and courage, strength and hope in the midst of them.

The motive or motives chiefly impelling Judas to his treachery may have been one or more of those I have mentioned, or perhaps something else altogether. Whatever it was that drove him to it, and however good and valid his reasons may have appeared at the time, once the deed was done Judas was full of remorse. But it was too late; he could not undo what he had done.

Whenever we are tempted to play Christ false, we should remember that someday we will look directly

into his eyes and have to recall then what we did and
how much it must have hurt him.

Someone musing on the betrayal from Judas's point
of view, once put these words into the traitor's mouth:

> They called Him King; and I would have no King:
> Let all be equal, ay, let none be best.
> Why should the weakling John be ever pressed
> Against His bosom, Peter urged to fling
> His clumsy zeal about, while I must bring
> Forsooth, the bag behind, and feed the rest,
> Never be praised, nor flattered nor caressed,
> Although so watchful in my stewarding?
> They called Him 'Son of God'. In rage I saw
> This vain idolatry. Was I not wise,
> Not honest, not in truth administering
> The holy precepts of our sacred law...?
>
> O, God! Those pleading, tender earnest eyes!
> Oh, God! Oh, God! Why did I do this thing?

Caiaphas

For a period of time Judas Iscariot held the centre of the passion drama stage, but soon that central position of his was taken over by Joseph Caiaphas the high priest. Once Judas had planted his traitor's kiss on Jesus's cheek, he moved into the background and Caiaphas moved to the front of the action.

As high priest, Caiaphas was officially the religious leader of the Jewish nation and he occupied this office from AD 18 to AD 36. This period of tenure was highly significant. Since the middle of the previous century the office of high priest had been an appointment of the Roman authorities, for the Romans were in military occupation of Palestine. As was inevitable, the Romans were anxious always to have a high priest who would co-operate readily and well. During this period of Roman occupation the average length of time for a high priest to remain in office was no more than four years. The fact that Caiaphas survived for no less than eighteen years speaks for itself. It shows just how satisfactory and zealous a collaborator the Romans must have found him.

It was this Caiaphas who headed the campaign for the elimination of Jesus. He led that campaign ruthlessly and he pursued it to its bitter end, to Calvary and its cross. Caiaphas more than any other individual was the cause of Jesus finishing up impaled on that terrible Roman agency of execution on the first Good Friday.

Yet Caiaphas was the *high priest*. He was the very one who was the religious leader of God's chosen people; and still it was he who was chiefly instrumental in engineering the murder of God's own son.

There can be few more startling illustrations than this that the best of religious opportunities, and the highest of religious privileges, are in themselves no guarantee that a man will have spiritual insight or spiritual vision – or even that he will decide to be a Christian and so make his own possession that abundant life which Jesus offers freely and lovingly to all who will accept it.

John Bunyan says at the close of *Pilgrim's Progress*, 'Then I saw that there was a way to Hell, even from the gates of Heaven.' So it is that some who dwell in the very neighbourhood of the new life Jesus has to give – for example, those who belong to Christian homes, or who attend church with some regularity – some of these, too, may miss the best of what Jesus has to give. Position and privilege are in themselves no guarantee of salvation. Commitment to Christ alone guarantees that.

Caiaphas's main personal involvement in the murder of Jesus was in his presiding at the trial before the Sanhedrin, the Jewish council. As a trial, Jesus's appearance before the Sanhedrin was a bit of a farce, riddled as it was with illegalities and injustices. Caiaphas, as president of the council, must carry the chief responsibility for that.

The Jews prided themselves on their justice and they had every right to do so. Their legal system was deliberately and carefully weighted in favour of the accused and was calculated to ensure that every man brought to trial would not only have full justice, but the benefit of any doubt that might be going. Nevertheless, in item after item, the Sanhedrin trying Jesus ignored its own very definite regulations.

It was, for instance, illegal for the Sanhedrin to convene during the hours of darkness; it was illegal for it to conduct a criminal case at all during the Passover;

it was illegal even to confirm, far less to carry out, an adverse sentence before the lapse of at least twenty-four hours from the end of the trial; it was illegal to make direct interrogation of the prisoner. Yet all these things were done – and we could go on. There were many illegal features of this so-called trial over which Caiaphas presided. I draw your attention to two of these.

For one thing, the trial before Caiaphas was not the open investigation a trial was meant to be. Instead, it was a matter of seeking confirmation for a decision and for a verdict that had already been decided. Caiaphas had his mind made up that Jesus should die and nearly all of the Sanhedrin were in agreement with him. In consequence the trial was in the main a frantic search for some grounds of accusation against Jesus that might afford justification for having him put to death.

We might consider that this kind of procedure was abominable. Indeed it was, but we should ask ourselves if we have any real right to throw stones of condemnation. It is by no means uncommon in our day – just as in any other day – for someone to prejudge Christ and then to seek to rationalise that verdict somehow. It may be when a man is confronted with Christ's call to repentance and faith; it may be when, already a committed Christian, he is presented with some challenge in Christ's name. In any event, he decides that he cannot and will not follow – and then searches for plausible reasons to support his rejection of Jesus.

He is well aware that to say 'yes' when Jesus calls is going to involve him in some cost and self-sacrifice, and he is just not prepared to give what is asked. But he will rarely be found to admit this. Instead, he cloaks his refusal with other alleged reasons, 'How can I follow Christ when I do not understand him fully? How can I follow when I have doubts about Christian belief and misgivings about the Bible? How can I follow when there is so much in the world and in the church that puzzles and perplexes me?'

The second illegal feature of the trial to which I wish to draw special attention is the fact that Caiaphas refused to allow any defence. He, as president of the court, was supposed to ensure that if there was anything at all that could be said in the prisoner's favour, then it should be made public. Far from encouraging any such testimony, Caiaphas flatly refused to allow the opportunity for any kind of favourable witness to be given.

We know that there were at least two members of that assembly who, however secretly, were favourably disposed to Jesus. These were Joseph of Arimathaea and Nicodemus. Surely any defence would have been telling. Surely any account, for example, of how Jesus had helped so many people must have made an impact on any fair-minded listener.

It may well be that, apart from Joseph and Nicodemus, few, if any, in that company were prepared at that time to be fair-minded where Jesus was concerned. But Caiaphas was taking no chances and no opportunity was given for any testimony in the prisoner's favour.

To this day it frequently happens that when Jesus is on trial at the bar of man's sympathies he is not allowed to plead.

There was a judge once, so the story goes, who listened as the prosecution stated its case but when the defence began to plead, he intervened, 'I do not want to hear any more. I used to listen to both sides of a case, but I found it only confused me. So now I listen to one side only.'

That was how it was with Caiaphas and the Sanhedrin; and that is how it often is still. Time after time Jesus Christ is condemned again without being properly heard. If we are ever like that, we are really much worse than Caiaphas. For we have all the additional testimony of the cross and the resurrection. Once we let these great events speak to our hearts and minds, once we look squarely at Jesus crucified and risen for love of us, surely we will not refuse to follow wherever he might lead.

At any rate the trial before Caiaphas ran through to its inevitable close. That Caiaphas would eventually have his way was never in any doubt. 'He is guilty of blasphemy', was the verdict. 'He must die', was the sentence.

A few hours later Jesus was dead. One of the most poignant elements in a most poignant drama was that, in killing Jesus, Caiaphas and his henchmen were killing the very Messiah, the anointed one of God, for whose coming they professed to be longing and praying so fervently.

The prophets had long foretold that God would send a saviour to his people and Caiaphas and the other priests made out that they were yearning for his coming. But here he had come in the person of Jesus and they did not and would not recognise him. Instead they crucified him.

They failed to recognise him because he was different from what they either wanted or expected. Their hopes and expectations were of a warrior prince who by force of arms would free their country from oppression and set up a wonderful new temporal state. In Jesus, however, the Messiah came as a man of peace whose only weapons were the weapons of love. Jesus was certainly bent on conquest as they expected the Messiah to be, but it was the conquest of men's hearts that he was after and the surrender of their lives that he sought.

Caiaphas and his party did not want a Messiah like this. They simply would not have him; and so they had him crucified.

Every day Jesus is crucified afresh simply because

men do not and will not recognise that in him is the fulfilment of their highest hopes and the meeting of their deepest needs. They cry out for freedom and happiness and self-expression and hope and satisfaction. These are the very things that Christ can give to those who will trust and follow him. But a great many people look on him as the enemy of these things – and so they send him to Calvary all over again.

When Jesus stood on trial before him, Caiaphas said to the Sanhedrin, 'What is your opinion?' 'He is guilty', they replied, 'He must die.'

Everyone who is confronted with Jesus is also confronted with that very question. No more important question is ever his to answer.

The Apostle Peter

Peter's dramatic part in the passion narrative began to be played in the upper room at the last supper. Jesus had been giving some final instructions and some final words of comfort to his disciples. He had a special word for Peter.

Peter, in his usual passionate style, had been making vehement declarations of unshakable loyalty. 'Lord', he protested, 'I am prepared to go to prison and even to the scaffold for you.' But Jesus knew his man. He knew also, as the others did not, just what lay ahead, and so he came out with the forecast, 'Ah, Peter, it is already dark, but I tell you that, before the cock crows to herald the dawn, you will deny that you even know me!'

Sure enough that was how it turned out. Within the hour came the agony of Jesus in Gethsemane. Then came the awful horror of the betrayal and in a moment Jesus was in the clutches of the Temple police and being hustled off none too gently to face Caiaphas and the Sanhedrin. When this happened the disciples were thrown into such consternation and fear that they broke and fled, all of them, that is, except Peter.

Peter was more adventurous than the rest and he followed in the wake of the crowd, although at a safe distance. He found it easy to slip unnoticed into the high priest's courtyard. There was so much noise and commotion. But, despite the large number of people milling around and the atmosphere of excitement that pervaded the whole scene, Peter's big bronzed figure was bound to draw attention before long. Stirrings of recognition were felt here and there. Surely this man had been seen in Jesus's company, had he not? And so Peter was challenged with being one of the Nazarene's friends. Challenged not just once or even twice, but three times. On every occasion Peter denied having had any association at all with Jesus and each successive time his denial was couched in stronger and more lurid terms.

Immediately after the third such incident a cock crowed and almost at the same moment Jesus was led through the hallway. As he passed, he halted for a moment, turned his head and caught Peter's eye. At once their recent conversation came back to Peter's mind, every single word of it. Filled with bitter regret and heart-rending remorse, he stumbled out into the darkness to weep for sorrow.

The story of Peter's three-fold denial of Jesus after his arrest is not only one of the most vivid in the New Testament but also one of the best known. It may, however, be of some value to look more particularly at several of its features.

For one thing, it is perfectly plain that the reason behind the denial was the *cost of being loyal*. Peter was well aware what it would mean for him to admit himself to be a follower of the hated Jesus. That crowd in its present murderous mood would give short shrift to anyone who claimed friendship with the carpenter-preacher from Nazareth.

Not so long ago Jesus had been the idol of the public but through the evil scheming of the priests, allied to the fickleness of human nature, all that had been changed. This same Jesus was generally regarded now with hate and with passion. To acknowledge a friendly connection with him was bound to mean, at very least, a rough time for Peter at the hands of the crowd, and perhaps a great deal worse.

The result was that Peter said emphatically, 'I do not even know the fellow.' Despite the promises he had made, despite the confidence he had felt, when it came to the point of crisis Peter abandoned Jesus.

It is still the case that, whenever one of his followers denies Jesus, it is basically because he counts the cost of loyalty too high. To be loyal to Jesus and to remain always loyal will frequently mean paying a heavy price – in terms perhaps of ridicule or of hostility or of self-sacrifice – and, even though he is aware that Jesus went to the cross for him, sometimes a man just will not pay that price.

Perhaps the most startling, and no doubt the most shocking, feature of Peter's denial is the manner in which his protestations became more violent each time, until in the end he was actually resorting to blasphemy in order to convince his hearers that he had no truck with Jesus.

Sometimes it may happen with some of us, too, that we are so afraid or so ashamed to own our allegiance to Jesus that we stoop lower and lower in an endeavour to convince others that our religion really rests lightly upon us. Rather than stand up openly for the one who died on a cross to save us, we resort to less and less Christlike things in order to disarm suspicions and show our neighbours and colleagues that, even though we carry the tag of Christian and church member, we are in fact no different from them – just as worldly, just as materially-minded, just as much creatures of sin.

We ought not to forget that Jesus said once that it will be impossible for him to acknowledge before God those who refuse to acknowledge him before their fellow-men.

There is something of arresting significance in this feature of the story, also, that the disciple who so poignantly denied Jesus was the very one who only a short time previously had vehemently promised his unswerving loyalty. 'Whatever it may cost me', he had said, '*I* will never let you down.' And yet here, only a short time later, he was denying his master three times over.

It may be that Peter's very pride and over-confidence contributed to his downfall. Paul has a striking warning in his first letter to the Corinthians when he says, 'If you feel sure that you are standing firm, beware' (*1 Corinthians* 10: 12). It is often when a man is most sure of himself, most confident of his loyalty, that some unexpected temptation breaks through his defences and lays him low.

In the business of Christian living a man must always be on his guard against pride and over-confidence. When in humility we are relying on the strength of Jesus and not on our own unaided resources, it is then that we are safest.

So far, this glance at Peter's part in the passion story has seen nothing but a tale of unrelieved gloom and sadness. We ought not to turn away from it, however, without recalling that there was a glorious and happy sequel. Even though that sequel properly belongs to the next part of our study – the Easter story – I can scarcely avoid referring to it here as well. For in the end the sun broke through the clouds and Peter took up again his extravagant promises and fulfilled them wonderfully well.

In his usual impetuous fashion Peter had declared himself willing to endure imprisonment and even to face death for his master. Later on he did just that. After many years of valiant service for Christ and his gospel, he was crucified to death for the sake of his faith.

The explanation for what may appear an almost incredible transformation is to be found in one of the loveliest of all the gospel narratives. Peter was overcome with remorse and grief after his eyes met those of Jesus in the courtyard of Caiaphas's palace. He would dearly have liked the opportunity to say 'sorry' to Jesus but the opportunity never came and Jesus was put to death.

Then came the resurrection and one day Peter found himself face to face with his Lord again. It was on the shores of Lake Galilee and Peter this time was totally unable to look into Jesus's face. But no word of rebuke came from the master's lips, no 'I told you so' or 'Why did you do it?' There was no mention of the past at all. Instead, simply and quietly, Jesus asked, 'Peter, do you love me?'

Brokenly, and on the verge of tears, the penitent disciple whispered back, 'Lord, you know that I love you.' In response Jesus said, 'Feed my sheep.' Three times over this happened and Peter knew, unbelievable as it might seem, that he was forgiven. He knew that, despite that terrible let down in Caiaphas's courtyard, Jesus was still prepared to trust him for the future.

In these circumstances what choice did Peter have but to do his very best to live up to that trust – and right well did he do it.

The story of Peter and his denial is in many ways similar to the story of us all. We so often let Jesus down, and sometimes very badly. Always, however, Jesus continues to love us, with a stubborn love that refuses to grow tired of us, a love that will gladly forgive us and afford us a new beginning. In face of such a love what can we give except our very best?

Andrew
(*John* 12: 2–33)

Andrew makes a significant appearance in the gospel narrative immediately prior to Good Friday, and although he appears only on two other occasions he comes through as a striking figure. When he takes the stage during Holy Week we find him introducing others to Jesus; and no action was more characteristic of Andrew than this.

On all three occasions that the gospels mention him Andrew is engaged on the very same pursuit of introducing others to Jesus. The first time he appears we find him introducing his own brother Simon (*John* 1: 40–42). Andrew had found someone and something so good that he wanted to share them first of all with his own family. In his second appearance (*John* 6: 8–10) Andrew is introducing a boy whose modest picnic lunch of five small loaves and two little fishes Jesus was able to use for the feeding of five thousand people. Jesus needed help in a crisis and Andrew brought to him someone who was able to supply that very help and at the same time found his meagre resources utilised beyond his wildest dreams. And now as the passion approached he came across some who had an interest in Jesus derived at second-hand and arranged to have them meet Jesus face to face.

Tradition represents Andrew as a far-travelled missionary for Jesus, taking the gospel to India and carrying it at length to Scotland. We cannot know whether there is any truth behind either of these traditions or not; but there is no doubting the fact that

Andrew was a dedicated missionary for Christ. Three times only he features in the gospel story and on each occasion he is actively engaged in bringing other people to Jesus.

It seems quite probable that Andrew did carry the good news to foreign parts, but even had he remained always on his native soil he must surely have been a missionary still. He was clearly a disciple who grasped every opportunity to point others to his master. It is, therefore, no surprise to discover that Andrew is not only the patron saint of Scotland, but also the patron saint of missionary workers the world over.

His example of constant evangelising for Christ has something to say to us all. He was not content to tell his loved ones about the difference Jesus's friendship was making to him; he wanted them to share its happiness. He was not content to have a committee meeting with the other disciples to discuss what could be done in the future about feeding the hungry; he wanted to enlist in Jesus's service whoever might be of immediate assistance. He was not content to educate the enquiring Greeks in matters of theology; he wanted them to have a personal meeting with Jesus.

Andrew was always anxious to be a witness to his faith. Now, the Greek word for 'witness' is *martus*, *marturos*, and it is the same word as 'martyr'. This is particularly interesting in the case of Andrew since, according to tradition, he was in the end martyred for his witnessing to Christ. Tradition says that because of his faith he was crucified to death on the x-shaped cross which bears his name today. Faithful in life to Jesus, Andrew remained faithful in death, too. Because he was faithful unto death he was also, of course, faithful unto life. That was the way Marget Howe would have expressed it, and that is what our Christian belief declares. (I suppose I ought not even to mention Marget Howe, far less to quote her story, because it belongs to

the Scottish 'kailyard' literature which is long out of
fashion and much despised by critics. I must confess,
however, to having a soft spot for some at least of the
discredited kailyard literature so let me introduce you to
Marget.)

She appears in Ian Maclaren's *Beside the Bonnie
Brier Bush*, where her son, George, is the schoolboy
genius of Drumtochty village. George goes off to
Edinburgh to study for the ministry and has a glorious
academic career, culminating in a double first honours
degree. But his health fails, and laden with honours as
he is, he comes home, aged twenty-three, to die. As his
life ebbs slowly away, George and his mother fall to
talking one day in their rose-filled garden – about
Edinburgh and his prizes and their broken dreams.

Marget's heart is full of pain but it is full of gladness,
too, because her son has all along kept faith with Christ,
and she says to him, 'Ye've been a good soldier, George,
and faithfu'.' And George, a little wistfully replies, 'Unto
death, ah'm dootin', mother.' 'Na, na', replies Marget,
'Unto life.'

So it was; and so it was with Andrew; and so it
always is. Whoever bears Christ's cross, whether it
means living or dying, will also wear his crown.

Let me employ a little more Greek. The name
Andrew is derived from the Greek for 'man' *aner,
andros. Anthropos* is man in the generic sense, a member
of the human race, which includes both male and
female; but *aner* means a male member of the species.
By definition, therefore, 'Andrew' means a real man.

What we know of Andrew shows that he bore the
name fittingly. Not just because of what we have
already noted, but even more for the fact that Andrew
showed himself to be a big man in the best sense. He
was large-minded and big-hearted, without any of that
pettiness in his nature which spoils so many of us.

Andrew, you see, was one of Jesus's earliest disciples,

and then had to watch while others took precedence over him. Yet he showed no resentment.

Andrew had previously been a follower of John the Baptist and that was how he made his first acquaintance with Jesus. He was much impressed and this led to a friend and himself having a long conversation with Jesus in the privacy of his room that lasted well into the night. As a result of this Andrew's heart was won completely and his allegiance never wavered until the day he died.

Andrew, then, was a member of Jesus's disciple band before most of the others, certainly before his brother Simon, later called Peter. It was Andrew indeed who was instrumental in bringing Jesus and Simon together in the first instance. And then he had to remain more or less in the background while his brother came more and more prominently to the front. Andrew, who had been there before him and without whom Peter might never have been there at all, had to stand by and watch his brother admitted to a closer intimacy with Jesus than ever was granted to him.

Most men in these circumstances would have given way to deep resentment and bitter jealousy. Not Andrew. He was just glad that the Master's work was being done, no matter who might be getting the more glamorous or more public jobs to do. His concern was not for his own position in the team but that the team should be functioning as effectively as possible.

You have to be a big man to be like that. Andrew was such a man. He showed no trace whatsoever of the envy or rancour which would have been so understandable. He was too big a man for that and was able to rise above such things. His was manhood of the greatest and most glorious kind. The secret was that Andrew was Christ's man through and through; and this is a secret we each may make our own.

Pontius Pilate

Caiaphas and his henchmen had decided that Jesus should die and they were in no doubt that he should; but they did not possess the power to have his execution carried out. Palestine was an occupied country and, while the occupying Roman power permitted a certain measure of self-government to the Jewish Sanhedrin, it kept the matter of capital punishment firmly within its own control.

The only exception made was in the case of a Gentile trespassing into that part of the Jewish Temple area which was prohibited to him. In such an instance the Romans allowed the Jewish authorities to pass and to execute the death sentence which their law clearly laid down as the punishment for this offence. In all other instances sentence of death could be passed only by the Procurator of Judaea who at this time was Pontius Pilate.

In consequence, once they came to the end of his trial before the Sanhedrin, Caiaphas and the others had to take Jesus to their Roman overlord and attempt to persuade him to agree that the carpenter-preacher should be executed.

In the gospels we have four reporters providing information about this occasion when Jesus stood trial for his life before Pilate. None of them gives, or seeks to give, an exhaustive account of the proceedings, but put together they present a fairly full picture. That picture is largely that of a man trying to run away from the decision which he is compelled to make concerning Jesus. As we read through these memoirs of the trial we get the strange but clear impression that it is, after all, not Jesus but Pilate who is on trial, in much the same way as, when you and I are confronted with a decision to make concerning Jesus, it is we who are on trial rather than he.

After Gethsemane and Judas, after Caiaphas and the Sanhedrin, Jesus was hauled before Pilate by the Jewish authorities backed by the mob. Their purpose was to seek from the procurator that sentence of death upon Jesus which only he could pass. Pilate listened to the recital of charges levelled against Jesus and then withdrew to interview the accused man in private.

It is clear that from the outset this humble peasant from Nazareth made an extraordinary impression on the man who was the most powerful individual in the whole land. So extraordinary was this impression that the governor felt himself in the grip of a strange and frightening impulse. His heart seemed almost to want to pay homage to this nonentity who stood before him as an accused criminal.

It did not take Pilate long to sift through the accusations brought against Jesus. He saw plainly that they contained no real substance and that Jesus was innocent of any crime. Returning to public view, he announced to the crowd that he had found no crime in Jesus and proposed to have him liberated. This intimation aroused such a frenzy of displeasure that Pilate, with fatal weakness, was led to reconsider his decision.

The trouble so far as Pilate was concerned was that he was afraid of what popular reaction might accomplish. Pilate had had a stormy career since he was appointed in AD 26 as procurator of the stormy province of Judaea; and already on three separate occasions he had been involved in a head-on clash with the Jews.

To begin with, unlike his predecessors in office, Pilate

had refused to permit his soldiers to remove the images from their standards on entering Jerusalem. The Roman military standards were poles carrying either an eagle or a representation of the emperor. The Jews, of course, regarded all images as an affront to God and for such things to be carried into their holy city was a terrible offence to them.

Aware of this and sensitive to the probable reaction if they acted otherwise, previous procurators had their legionaries take the images from their standards before entering Jerusalem. Pilate however, seems to have been lacking in their sensitivity or their diplomacy, and he insisted that his troops march in with the standards untouched. Great offence was caused and a deputation of Jews waited on Pilate to discuss the matter with him. He refused to see them but they obstinately refused to abandon their purpose and waited on for five days, even though Pilate threatened to put them to death. In the end Pilate was forced to yield and to concede their point.

Pilate's second occasion of head-on conflict with the Jewish people occurred when he erected on the walls of Herod's palace (where the procurator normally resided when in Jerusalem) certain golden shields bearing the name of the emperor. This was regarded as an attempt to introduce Caesar-worship which was already flourishing elsewhere in the empire. So seriously was this taken and so strongly did the Jews feel about it that they sent a delegation all the way to the Emperor Tiberius in Rome with a complaint and an appeal. The emperor heard their delegation favourably and sent orders to Pilate that the practice was to be discontinued.

These two instances of Pilate clashing with the Jewish people and their feelings were due in large measure, it would seem, to a perverse streak in the man's make-up. Convinced that what they regarded as religious principles of paramount importance were in fact no more than foolish prejudices, Pilate tried to ride roughshod over them and rode headlong into trouble as a result.

His next occasion of offence and conflict had a different kind of origin. It arose out of an attempt to effect something which was both wise and beneficial, if not indeed necessary. Pilate decided that Jerusalem ought to have an improved water supply. So he set about having a new aqueduct constructed. That was fine but the trouble was that, in order to pay for this highly commendable project, he simply extracted the money from the Temple treasury. The high-handed nature of this action, allied to the unacceptable fact that it was devoting to a secular purpose money which was designated for religious purposes only, meant that once again great offence was caused. As a matter of fact it sparked off a riot which was put down only after much blood was shed.

Pilate was only too well aware that with this kind of record behind him he could not afford to risk another confrontation. Should there be any more trouble in Judaea, and should word of it reach the emperor's ears, it would not matter much where the rights and wrongs of the affair lay. Pilate knew that it would almost certainly mean the end of his career and perhaps even of his life.

Pilate found himself, therefore, in a great dilemma. He had no doubt that Jesus was completely innocent of the charges brought against him and he was much impressed by the man personally, so that he very much wanted to let Jesus go free. At the same time he could not forget that the people who were pressing for the death penalty were the very people who held his own destiny in their hands.

In an attempt to resolve his dilemma, Pilate tried several expedients.

Recalling that Herod, Tetrarch of Galilee, was also in

Jerusalem at that time, Pilate sent Jesus along to him. The accompanying message expressed the governor's compliments to the tetrarch and went on to say that since Jesus came from Galilee and since Herod had, under Rome, a measure of jurisdiction over that area, Pilate was assigning the disposal of Jesus's case, as a matter of courtesy, to him.

Pilate hoped that in this way he might extricate himself from the horns of his dilemma; but his plan failed. It was not for nothing that Herod had been given the nickname of 'fox'. His cunning was more than a match for Pilate's wiles. Before very long the guard-escort was back with the prisoner and with a note from Herod to say that he appreciated Pilate's gesture very much but he would not dream of usurping what was properly the procurator's place. He was returning Jesus with thanks for Pilate to pass judgment.

Pilate attempted to 'pass the buck' but it did not work. Are not you and I sometimes guilty of trying the same kind of method of evading our responsibilities with regard to Jesus?

Thwarted in his first plan, Pilate resorted to another. It was an established custom that, at the time of the Jewish Passover festival, the Roman governor should release a state prisoner as a gesture to the subject native populace. It so happened that there was in custody at that time a particularly notorious and dangerous character called Barabbas. 'I know what I will do', thought Pilate, 'I will remind the people of the custom and offer to release either Barabbas or Jesus. They cannot possibly choose to have such a man as Barabbas set free.'

But, spurred on by the priests, that is just what they did and so Pilate was once again defeated in his attempt to evade the responsibility of decision concerning Jesus. In any event, even if he had succeeded it would have been an unsatisfactory solution to his problem. It would still have been a refusal on Pilate's part to come out on Jesus's side and that would have been virtually equivalent to bringing in a verdict against him.

It is very like that in our own time, and so far as we ourselves are concerned. Failure to make a choice in favour of Jesus comes to the same thing as bringing in a verdict against him. Yet so often when a man is confronted with Jesus he tries to do a Pilate and evade his responsibility of decision. 'What about so-and-so? How is he going to decide?' Always the verdicts to be brought in concerning Jesus are verdicts we must bring in for ourselves whatever others may be doing. To shirk the issue is usually to condemn Jesus and so to condemn ourselves.

Pilate next tried to find escape along the avenue of compromise. In a rather pathetic endeavour to do the right thing by Jesus, and at the same time to avoid offending the Jews, he suggested that the prisoner might be flogged and then released. The mob simply would not have it. Only Jesus's death was going to satisfy them. In any case, such a compromise would also have been virtually equivalent to a verdict against him.

Often today a compromise where Jesus is concerned is equivalent to a verdict against him. Jesus himself tells us plainly that we cannot serve two masters. When a man attempts a compromise – perhaps giving to Jesus lip-service but to something else his true devotion – he is sending Jesus once more to the cross.

How was Pilate to escape now? What he might have done next we will never know, for suddenly and dramatically the issue was decided for him.

All this time, as Pilate vacillated, the crowd had been growing more restive. Now, as the governor stood once more in the throes of indecision, a voice rang out loud and clear: 'If you let this man go, you are no friend to Caesar.' Pilate may well have stiffened as if struck, for the threat was obvious. For him to acquit Jesus would ensure that a complaint would wing its way swiftly to Rome, and he knew only too well what that would entail. No matter how unjustified that might be, Pilate simply could not survive another complaint to the emperor. And so his mind was made up and he passed the death sentence on Jesus.

Even with the decision taken and the sentence passed, Pilate made a last desperate attempt to free himself from blame. In full view of the assembled crowd he called for a bowl of water and went through a ritual of washing his hands as a sign that he was disclaiming any responsibility for the death of this innocent man. But Pilate was unable to wash away the guilt of his part in Jesus's murder just by washing his hands. The final decision that Jesus should die was his decision, as it could only be. No plea of circumstances could alter that fact.

Yet this is often the kind of excuse that is offered today. A man maintains that it is not lack of desire but adverse circumstances that keep him back, whether it be a question of taking the great decision to be a Christian or going regularly to worship or keeping a vow or fulfilling a promise. It is, however, no real excuse, where Christ and his service are concerned, to plead force of circumstances or difficulty of conditions. Jesus makes it plain that decision for him will involve us in cost and sacrifice. He also makes it plain that we must continue to follow, whatever the difficulties, for in that alone is to be found life at its best, both for this world and for the world to come.

'What shall I do with Jesus called Christ?' was the great question that faced Pilate. It is the most important question that anyone is ever called upon to answer.

Simon of Cyrene

Sometimes in a play there is a character with a minor role who makes an impression out of all proportion to the size of his part. He is on the stage only for a short time and yet he leaves such a mark on your memory that, when you look back, you think not only of the play itself or of the principals but also of him. When the greatest drama of all time was being played out in Jerusalem, one character appeared for little more than an instant, but is remembered for ever. He was a man who stumbled into the action and was swept into glory.

It was the morning of the first Good Friday and Jesus was going out to die. The iniquitous trial was over, the farcical verdict had been given, the shocking judgment had been passed and now the sentence was being carried out.

The custom was that a man condemned to die, as Jesus was, carried part of his cross to the place of execution – the *patibulum* or cross-beam. This custom was observed in Jesus's case, too, but Jesus was in a very weak physical condition. He had been up all night with neither food nor sleep, he had been subjected to gruelling cross-examination and constant strain. All of this had taken severe toll of his resources and at the end of it all he had undergone the Roman punishment of flagellation. This was a flogging with a many-thonged whip, each of whose thongs was studded with pieces of sharp metal and bone designed to lift the flesh from the body. Many men died under this scourging and, on top of all that had gone before, it must have left Jesus very close to death.

The upshot was that, with his physical strength so severely weakened, Jesus found the weight of the cross too much for him to carry any distance. The execution procession had not gone very far before his knees buckled beneath his burden, and it was immediately obvious that he would not be able to carry it any farther.

This development posed a pretty problem for the officer in charge of the execution squad. The *patibulum* had to be got to the place of execution but none of his soldiers could be asked to demean himself by carrying it.

By law he was entitled to conscript a civilian into service and he could, therefore, impress any man from the crowd into being a cross-bearer for the occasion. In the present circumstances, however, this would be a risky thing to do. Not only were feelings running high against Jesus but the Jews had a great horror of coming into contact with any dead person or any of the trappings of death. To force a Jew in that crowd, especially at the most sacred Passover season, to touch such an object as an execution cross was to invite serious trouble.

As the officer cast his eyes round the throng, wondering how he could resolve his problem, his gaze fell on a coloured man, a North African by all appearances. This was clearly a visitor to Jerusalem, a pilgrim come to the holy city for the Passover. Here was the answer. He would conscript this stranger. That should be safe enough.

That was how it happened that Simon from Cyrene in Libya became the man who carried Jesus's cross to Calvary; and with that he stepped into a permanent place in history's hall of fame.

It is surely deeply moving and significant that the man to whom history entrusted the task of carrying to Calvary the cross on which Jesus was to die, a task then of shame but now of glory, was a man whose skin was probably black. What better reminder could there be that, when Jesus died, he died for all. The corollary is that, if we know Jesus, it is for every man, whatever his race or colour, that we should seek to live.

The task imposed on Simon was one which he would never have chosen of his own accord. Yet it is by this and this alone that the world knows him and for this that the Christian world cherishes his memory with affection.

How much would any Christian today be prepared to give for the privilege of carrying his Lord's cross to Calvary; but it was counted no privilege by Simon, not at the time anyway. He was resentful of the imposition, aggrieved that he should be the one unlucky enough to be singled out, cursing the bad luck that had brought him to that particular spot at that particular time and so involved him in such shame and notoriety.

In the event, of course, his misfortune became the greatest honour of his life and his enforced humiliation its greatest glory.

It can often turn out with us, too, that what at the time we consider to be a misfortune turns out to be a blessing. There is no doubt that the blessings of God sometimes come to us veiled in thick disguise. What is more, frequently things which are full of hurt and shame and distress can be made into things of benefit and even of glory. Faith in Christ and continuing trust in him in face of everything are a spiritual alchemy that is able to transform even the bleakest of life's experience into gold.

Simon was not a follower of Jesus when this incident occurred and probably knew little or nothing about him. But it seems that shortly afterwards he must have become a follower. How this happened we are not told, but we can guess. Close personal contact with Jesus at this highly dramatic point could not fail to impress Simon greatly and the impact of Jesus's personality upon him must have been tremendous. No doubt he lingered at Golgotha to watch the end and so looked on Jesus in all the noble majesty of his dying. The consequence was that he would go away from the scene grieving at the waste of so fine a young life and lamenting that once more, as so often, wrong had triumphed over right and evil men had won the day.

Soon, however, an incredible story reached his ears. There was a report circulating in the streets that Jesus had been raised from the dead and was alive again. It had to be nonsense, of course, but Simon's natural curiosity was heightened by his own involvement in the affair and he felt compelled to look further into it. And he did. To his amazement he discovered that the report of Jesus's resurrection was so well substantiated that it must be true. No other explanation met the facts. In consequence Simon was won to Jesus's side.

Simon's conversion may not have happened exactly like that, although it is not at all unlikely that it did. But what matters is that somehow it did happen, and after it did, Simon became an ardent missionary for his Lord, Not only in the meeting-place, not only at the street corner but also, and first and foremost, in his own home – the most difficult, and yet the most important, place to witness. Simon brought his own sons, Alexander and Rufus, to Jesus.

Nicodemus and Joseph of Arimathaea
(*Mark* 15: 42–47)

Nicodemus and Joseph of Arimathaea were two men who did not show up very well in the beginning but turned up trumps at the end of the story. Theirs was in a way a story of failure that became success, a story of tragedy that became triumph.

We do not have much information about either of these men and they make only brief appearances in the pages of the New Testament. But their part in the story of Jesus is dramatic and moving.

Both were wealthy members of the Sanhedrin, the Jewish council or parliament of seventy members which controlled that generous measure of self-government which the Roman Empire had delegated to Palestine. Both were obviously wealthy as, on the one hand, Nicodemus was able to purchase expensive spices for the anointing of Jesus's body and, on the other hand, Joseph of Arimathaea provided his own expensive new tomb for Jesus's burial.

Joseph and Nicodemus, alike in these things mentioned, were alike also in something that from our point of view is much more interesting and much more meaningful. In relation to Jesus they each acted in similar fashion. During his lifetime they were drawn to him but lacked the courage to have this attraction made public. It was only after Jesus had been crucified that they came out into the open and acknowledged that they were on his side. Let us take a closer look at these events.

When Nicodemus came to see Jesus under cover of darkness, as is recorded in the third chapter of John's

gospel, it probably meant that already Nicodemus was
on the side of the young carpenter-preacher from
Nazareth. But it also indicates quite plainly that he was
not yet prepared to have it known. He did not want his
friends to learn of it, least of all his fellow members of
the Sanhedrin who as a body were already bitterly
antagonistic to Jesus. He was content, therefore, to keep
his discipleship secret.

Joseph of Arimethaea does not appear on the gospel
narrative scene until after the crucifixion but when he
does, the fourth evangelist makes it quite specific that
he, like Nicodemus, had been content to keep his
discipleship a purely private matter, content to be 'a
secret disciple' (*John* 19: 38). Even when Jesus stood on
trial for his life and Joseph and Nicodemus were two of
the seventy who must decide his fate, they maintained
their silence. As the flood of hostility and hate rose
higher and became ever more certain to sweep Jesus to
a totally undeserved death, they made not the slightest
attempt to stem it. As false testimonies and distortions
were piled one on top of the other in search of a guilty
verdict against the man they acknowledged in their
hearts as master, they failed to say one single word in
his favour.

Joseph and Nicodemus did not even break their
silence when the vote was taken and Jesus was
pronounced guilty and deserving of death. Rather than
come openly out on his side they let his enemies drag
him relentlessly on his way to the cross without once
opening their mouths in his defence.

What was the reason? John says that Joseph kept
quiet out of fear and this is probably correct in the case
of Nicodemus too. They were both afraid of the
consequences of being openly branded as followers of
Jesus; afraid of the hostility and scorn of friends and
colleagues; afraid of the cost in terms of popularity and
prestige, perhaps even of position.

At any rate they kept silent even when Jesus was so inexorably being hounded to his death by Caiaphas and the other members of the Sanhedrin. Of course they could have argued within themselves – and perhaps they did, who knows – that nothing they could say or do would alter the course of events. They could have said – and who could make out a contrary case – that their two voices and their two votes would not sway the verdict. They could have been persuaded – and the logic of the matter would be undeniable – that any protest on their part was utterly incapable of saving Jesus and might well severely harm themselves.

And yet who can say how much it might have meant to Jesus in that lonely, pain-filled night if only he had heard one voice raised on his behalf, if only he had been able to look on one face in that assembly and see there some friendship and the promise of some support. Joseph and Nicodemus could not have saved Jesus from the cross, that is true, but they could have brought him a degree of consolation and encouragement that might have been of immeasurable value to the Son of God as he braced himself for the ordeal of giving his life for the world.

But they kept silent or, perhaps, as some have suggested, took the easier way out, easier but just as hurtful to Jesus, and deliberately absented themselves from the meeting. It was only after the deed was done and their master was dead that they let it be known that they had been among those who acknowledged Jesus as leader.

There is a wealth of sadness in this, that they let Jesus go unsupported and undefended to his cross and then did their best to honour him after he was dead. It would have meant so much more to Jesus for them to give him open loyalty and courageous support during his lifetime, rather than to provide him with a magnificient burial place and fine grave clothes when he was dead.

People, more's the pity, have behaved in similar fashion towards their friends all down the centuries and they do it still. A single rose given in life is worth a great deal more than dozens of them sent to a funeral. A word of appreciation spoken during a man's lifetime is of far greater value than any number of fine orations over his corpse. There is a reminder here that we should pay as much tribute as we can and make as much grateful response as we may to those we love while they are alive, and not wait until they are dead before we express our gratitude to them.

At the same time, Joseph and Nicodemus did come good in the end. They did in the end take a stand openly for Jesus. The strange and somewhat ironic thing is that it really required much more courage then to declare themselves for Jesus than would have been required earlier. For now Jesus was dead. He was totally discredited and, in the minds of all, friend and foe alike, he and his cause were completely finished. To stand up in such circumstances and be counted for Jesus was brave to the point of being foolhardy.

Nevertheless, Joseph and Nicodemus did just that. Joseph went to the governor, obtained permission to take away Jesus's body for burial and supplied his own personal tomb for the purpose; Nicodemus purchased the materials necessary to prepare the body for burial; and together they carried out the melancholy duty of laying Jesus's body to rest. The men who had been afraid to be known as Jesus's followers when he was alive, now cast their cowardice aside and bravely stood up for him as soon as he was dead.

There are few more dramatic illustrations of the power of Jesus's cross than this. Jesus had forecast that his cross would be a force of compelling magnetism that would have an attraction for men the world over (*John* 12: 32). Already he was being proved right. What even the life of Jesus had been unable to do with Joseph and

Nicodemus, his death achieved at once. Within the hour their prudent fears were thrown aside and they paraded their Jesus colours for all to see.

The cross of Jesus turned cowards into brave men here. It has continued down the years to transform cowardice into courage. It still retains its ancient power and may make heroes even of us, given the opportunity.

There is one more comment to make. Jesus may well have been sore hurt by the failure of Joseph and Nicodemus to speak up for him in earlier times and especially when he was undergoing his trial before the Sanhedrin. But he would also be aware of the different way they acted later and that must have meant a great deal to him then.

When we let a loved one slip away from this life without saying or doing all the things we might and should, the sad fact is that we have missed the boat so far as they are concerned. But no matter how much or how often we let down our crucified Lord, we always have the opportunity to make up for it in some measure for he is also now risen and alive. He is aware of all we are and all we do, conscious of our every repentance and our every endeavour to redeem past failures, and greatly gladdened by them.

Part of the glad tidings of the Christian gospel is that it is never too late for a fresh beginning.

PART III

People in the Easter Story

Thomas the Doubter

Everyone, I think, knows the story of how Jesus appeared to the apostles on the first Easter night in the absence of Thomas and they were joyfully convinced that he was indeed risen from the dead. When Thomas returned to the group, he flatly refused to believe their story. It was all nonsense, he was sure, because that kind of thing just did not happen; and so he vehemently declared that he would not believe unless he not only saw for himself but actually touched the wounds of crucifixion in Jesus's body. In the event, however, when the risen Jesus came back to the apostles with Thomas present, Thomas did not insist on touching the wounds. It was enough for him to see his Master alive again and at once he pledged his wholehearted belief and allegiance.

Thomas has come down the centuries wrapped in a good deal of infamy so far as many are concerned. He has been much despised and maligned. The very term 'doubting Thomas' which he has given to the language is an indication of the contempt in which he is generally held. I want to suggest that Thomas deserves a much better verdict than that. I am going to suggest, indeed, that Thomas can be both a rebuke and an inspiration to us. He certainly provides lessons for us all.

To begin with, I ask you to go back a bit in the gospel story and see Thomas displaying great *courage and devotion* on his Master's behalf. When Jesus insisted on making his way to Jerusalem or, at least, to its near vicinity, and the others were thrown into some disarray by this intention, it was Thomas who said, 'let us also go that we may die with him' (*John* 11: 16).

Jesus, in the eyes of his disciples, was clearly acting very foolishly, and obstinately running his head into serious trouble. He was courting disaster and inviting death, and Thomas was as glumly certain as the rest what the grim outcome must be if Jesus persisted. At the same time, he was bravely determined that, if Jesus was resolved to die, he for one would die by his side.

Thomas did not yet fully understand Jesus. He was in fact a long way short of that. But it is plain that he loved his leader very much and that, after all, is what counts the most. True devotion to Jesus is more important than proper doctrine or correct theology.

Now, do not misunderstand me. These things matter but they are not all-important. I think many Christians go through a phase where they reckon that the man who does not hold precisely what they see as the correct Christian beliefs must be damned, or very near to being damned. I certainly did; but I have come to see that a great many people who do not share my opinions about this or about that far outstrip me in terms of their devotion to Jesus. And this is always what counts most in the end.

As Robert Burns once put it:

> The heart's aye the pairt aye
> That mak's us richt or wrang.

Let me turn now to Thomas's *scepticism*. Supposing we take this simply at its face value, that is, as the reaction of an unwilling material mind to accept that the supernatural could have any reality in this world. Are we in any position to condemn? Is it not the case that most of us present-day Christians are just as fanatical devotees of the cult of 'seeing is believing' as Thomas appears to have been? Is it not so likely as to be almost certain that most of us, placed in the same position as Thomas, would have reacted in exactly the same fashion?

After all, try to visualise the situation. With the

crucifixion of their leader, all the hopes of the disciple band had been cruelly and completely crushed. The fine dreams they had come to cherish concerning Jesus were utterly ruined and they were enveloped in black despair and abject hopelessness. The day of the cross left them without the slightest thought of resurrection. Had Jesus not spoken of this? Indeed he had, but they had not even begun to understand what he was talking about.

For the disciples, as for every other person, the crucifixion of Jesus had written a total and irreversible 'finish' across his career; and Thomas entirely shared the mind of his fellow-disciples on this matter. The result was that, when he returned to them this first Easter evening and listened to them babbling away about seeing Jesus alive, he not surprisingly scoffed and declared his need for further proof before he could even begin to entertain such a preposterous idea. After all, since Thomas had been away, he probably did not even know about the empty tomb.

Anyway, Thomas wanted to be sure, and is there so very much wrong with that? We do well to seek to become surer and surer of the foundation of our faith and of the hope that is in us.

Perhaps there is more to Thomas's scepticism than appears on the surface. It may have been occasioned, to some extent at least, by the fact that the news he was hearing was such *good news*. Thomas may well have been afraid to let himself accept this report simply because of its joyous nature. Could such glad tidings possibly be true?

Many a man holds back today from accepting the resurrection gospel simply because he fears it is too good to be true. The Christian faith asserts that it is true and there is a great deal of solid evidence to back up that assertion. Jesus rose and Jesus lives; and he extends an open invitation to all and sundry to accept his daily friendship and so to share in his victory.

E

Whatever else we may think about him, Thomas turned up trumps in the end. Despite the blustering scepticism which provoked him to declare that you would never get him believing such a tale unless he could touch the very wounds of the cross, when the time came that the risen Jesus stood before him, he did none of the things he had said he must do. Instead he hailed Jesus at once, 'My Lord and my God.'

In this acknowledgment Thomas went much further than any of the others had yet gone in their attitude to Jesus. He was at one and the same time declaring that he believed Jesus to be divine and also pledging him his full, unreserved commitment. Once Thomas saw the risen Lord, there was no holding back.

He gave himself fully into Jesus's keeping that day and, if tradition is to be relied on to any degree whatsoever, he maintained that all-out loyalty to the end. Sceptical he had been, but once he was assured that the Lord had risen, there were no half-measures for Thomas in Christ's service. Nor should there be for any Christian. No half-measures sufficed for Jesus. He went all the way to Calvary for us.

Peter the Fisherman

Peter the fisherman was one of the characters we looked at in the passion story where he played a prominent part. Peter was prominent also in the post-resurrection story of Jesus and so rightly belongs to our present study, too.

First, we look back to the passion and give some thought to *Peter the failure*. When Jesus, shortly before the end, was warning his disciples of the sufferings that lay ahead and of the pressures to which they would, therefore, be subjected, it was Peter who said, 'No matter what the rest may do, I will never let you down, even if it means imprisonment, even if it means death.' But, of course, as all the world knows, when the moment of crisis came, Peter failed to stand by his extravagant boasts. Three times over he flatly denied that he even was acquainted with Jesus and the end of this drama within a drama saw him stumble out into the darkness weeping bitter tears of regret.

Peter's story here could so easily be our story, and often is. We make promises to Jesus and we really intend to stand by them; but so often we too fail when the crunch comes and the cost begins to bite. And all this despite the bitter price that he paid for love of us.

Second, we look at *Peter the forgiven*. After his threefold denial of Jesus in the courtyard of Caiaphas's palace, Peter was flung into the very depths of remorse and penitence. How much he would have given for the opportunity to tell Jesus how sorry he was that he had let him down. But the opportunity did not come and soon his leader was dying on a Roman cross.

Then came the glad transformation of the resurrection
and soon afterwards the risen Jesus met with seven of
his disciples on the shores of Lake Galilee (*John* 21).
They had been fishing on the sea and Jesus called them
ashore, assisting them as they came to make a gigantic
catch. That was when and how Peter came face to face
with Jesus again, for the first time since the three-fold
denial. He did not know where to look and found it
beyond him to meet Jesus's eyes.

To his intense astonishment there was no word of
rebuke from Jesus. No 'I told you so' or 'Why did you
do it?' Instead Jesus simply said to Peter softly and
tenderly, 'Peter, do you love me?' When Peter answered
that he did, Jesus said, 'Feed my sheep'. Three times
over this question and answer were repeated, just as
three times over Peter had denied all knowledge of his
Lord.

'Feed my sheep', said Jesus to Peter, and the disciple
knew that, astonishingly, he was restored and forgiven
and that all was well again with him and his Master. So
may it be with us. This, too, can be any man's story. If
he comes to Jesus in penitence after a failure, no matter
how terrible, there is always a new beginning to be had.

There is more to Peter's story even than this. Hard on
the heels of his restoration and forgiveness we see *Peter
the frail*. This disciple is not perfect yet, not by a long
way. The old man of human nature is not dead inside
him, not by a long chalk. The struggle, the disappoint-
ments, the heartbreaks, the failures are far from being
ended yet.

Peter is in the seventh heaven of happiness that Jesus
has taken him back and entrusted him with such
responsibility. But almost immediately after Jesus's com-
mission to him, Peter catches sight of John, the
favourite disciple, in the background. At once his old,
somewhat cantankerous, nature reasserts itself.
Petulantly he says to Jesus, 'And what about him? You

are laying tasks on my shoulders. What are you going to ask him to do?'

Jesus replies, 'Never mind what I have in store for him. You know perfectly well what *your* responsibility is and I am depending on you to see to it.'

Once more Peter's story could be our story, too. No doubt it often is. Like Peter we are in danger of becoming so concerned with what others are doing or are failing to do for Christ and his church that we are distracted from fulfilling our own commitment as well as we might. Like Peter we, too, may find ourselves saying, 'What about so-and-so? What is he doing? What is he giving? What contribution is he making in terms of his money or his time or his skill?'

With us, too, the old man is always fighting to reassert himself and to take us over again. Sometimes he succeeds, for we also are frail.

Some preachers might give the impression that, once a man decides to be a Christian, everything is fine and he will have no more worries. In a sense that is true. Once a man makes commitment of himself to Christ, in a very wonderful sense he has no need to worry about anything that may come his way. At the same time, he still has to contend with his basic (and sometimes base) human nature. At times, frequently perhaps, he will find that human nature takes over and knocks him off the straight path of Christian obedience.

There is, however, thank God, always the opportunity of another fresh start. Peter found that, and so may any one of us.

We may well see ourselves in Peter. When we fall, Jesus will pick us up again if we allow him. That will not be the end of it, of course. We will fall again; but Jesus will always be ready to keep picking us up and starting us afresh if we are willing.

The Two from Emmaus
(*Luke* 24: 13–35)

The story of Jesus's two followers from Emmaus and of what happened to them on the first Easter day is one of the most vivid and dramatic, and at the same time one of the most moving, in the whole Bible. Luke is the only one of the four evangelists who tells this story and he makes it come alive.

The Emmaus story raises two major questions which have occupied scholars to a great extent: the location of Emmaus, and the identity of the two followers. Despite the vast amount of scholarship and of thought applied to these two problems, there is still no certain answer to either.

Many of the places that feature in the gospels have had a continuing existence and are still easily and unmistakably identifiable today. Emmaus, however, is not one of these. Three suggestions in particular are made as to its location.

The Franciscans are the custodians of many Christian sites in the Holy Land and they identify the New Testament Emmaus with a place nowadays known as Kubebieh. It lies to the north of Jerusalem and its distance from the city fits in very well with the 'seven miles' mentioned in Luke's account. The Byzantines, on the other hand, due to an error in the gospel manuscripts that they used, took Emmaus to be one hundred and sixty, not sixty, furlongs from Jerusalem and consequently identified it with a place known today as Amwas, on the Jerusalem–Jaffa (Joppa) road. Some scholars think that their misreading of the text may after all have led them to the right answer.

The third most commonly proposed site for the Emmaus of the Easter story is the one that the Crusaders favoured. They located it at a village known today as Abu Ghosh which was the Kiryath-Yearim of the Old Testament, the place where the Ark of the Covenant once rested. No one can be sure if any of these suggested sites is the correct location, but when I lead a group to the Holy Land, I like to take them to Abu Ghosh. There I tell them that this may well be the very place where the risen Jesus was made known in the breaking of the bread on the first Easter Day.

Whether or not this is the fact of the matter we cannot tell, and may never know. Nevertheless Abu Ghosh, where the Crusaders coming in from the sea first caught sight of the outskirts of Jerusalem on the hilltops ahead, provides a fitting and impressive setting in its ancient Crusader church crypt for reading aloud Luke's Emmaus story and rejoicing especially in its exultant declaration, 'It is true; the Lord has risen.'

It is equally impossible to give a final and authoritative answer to the question, 'Who were the two followers of Jesus in the Emmaus story?' Despite the fact that they are featured much in Christian art, we do not know and cannot even guess with any great confidence who they were. It is not even certain whether they were two men or a man and his wife.

One was called Cleopas – that much we know from Luke's narrative – but his companion's identity is shrouded in mystery. One suggestion was that it might have been Peter, but the text really rules that out. It makes it clear that the two Emmaus travellers, whoever they were, were not part of 'the eleven', that is, the apostles. Whether it was Cleopas's wife or some unidentified male companion, no one knows.

Whoever they were, Cleopas and his friend had a quite marvellous experience on that first Easter afternoon and evening. Like all the rest of Jesus's friends, they had been plunged into the very depth of the blackest despair when their beloved master was put to death. All the high hopes and fine dreams that had centred round Jesus were now in ruins at their feet. They knew with a sickening sense of irretrievable finality that it was all over and their hearts were broken because of it. Some of the women in the group had come from the burial place that day with a garbled and unbelievable tale that Jesus's grave was empty, but they had not been able to make anything at all of that. In any case nothing could possibly alter the sad and awful fact that Jesus was dead.

They were still in this state of depression and be-wilderment when they set out from Jerusalem to make their way to Emmaus, some seven miles away. The 'stranger' who fell in with them on their journey went some way, by his conversation, to lift their spirits. But that was as nothing to the utter transformation that overtook them when they reached their home. They pressed their unknown companion to come in and share a meal with them. In the simple act of breaking bread he revealed to them that he was their own Jesus risen from the dead.

Even yet they could scarcely believe it. But it was unmistakably true. The clear evidence was before their very eyes. Gone at once was their depression and their sadness, and they were filled with exultation. So full of joy were they indeed that, once Jesus had taken his leave of them, nothing would stop them from hurrying back to Jerusalem, even at that late hour, despite the distance and their physical tiredness, to share with the others their wonderful discovery.

There are several aspects of the Emmaus disciples' experience that may be worth some reflection. Firstly, it was an experience that could be described as turning sunset into sunrise for them. It is more than possible that, physically speaking, they were walking into the sunset that afternoon. Certainly if Abu Ghosh is to be identified as Emmaus, these followers of Jesus were heading west as they left Jerusalem. It was already well into the afternoon and, since darkness falls around six o'clock in the Holy Land, the sun was already sinking into the horizon.

They may well, then, have been walking into the sunset in the literal sense. There is no doubt, however, that in the metaphorical sense the sun had already set for them; and the discovery that Jesus was risen brought them a bright new day. We are told that it was a regular practice before the coming of the Christian faith for graves to be made facing the west, symbol of nightfall and darkness. With the coming of Christ, graves were commonly made to face the east, symbol of the dawn and of new life.

All this symbolises the transforming news that the risen Jesus gives victory to those who follow him, not only over death but also over all the hurtful and spoiling things of life.

Secondly, Jesus cleared up a lot of problems for them that day. As they set out on their walk to Emmaus, apart from their great sadness at what they reckoned to be their irretrievable loss, they were considerably puzzled about many aspects of the recent events. As they walked along the road that afternoon, Jesus explained many things to them. He helped them to make sense of things, just as he can help us to make sense of things if we will let him.

Thirdly, he became recognisable to them in the action of the breaking of bread. Now, this was not the communion service, as has sometimes been suggested. The sacrament of the Lord's supper had only recently been instituted. It had not yet been celebrated after its institution and was, therefore, not yet a familiar procedure.

What opened wide the eyes of the Emmaus pair was

an ordinary action set in perfectly ordinary circumstances. This is surely a reminder that the presence of the risen Lord is not restricted to special occasions such as the communion service. The risen Jesus is beside us always and everywhere.

Fourthly, their eventual recognition of Jesus ultimately depended on their own decision. He did not force that recognition on them. He 'made as if to continue his journey'. It was because they pressed him to stay that the rest followed.

Jesus always respects the freedom of the individual. He never forces himself or his help, nor even his salvation, upon us. He always waits for a man to say, 'Please come in'.

Fifthly, once they knew that Jesus was risen, these disciples from Emmaus wanted nothing better than to tell others this marvellous news. They had to share it. They found it quite impossible to keep it to themselves.

That is how it must be with all of us who come to know the risen Christ. It is too good a thing to keep to ourselves and so we must be announcing it to the world by our words and by our lives so that others, too, may come to know and to say, 'It is true: the Lord has risen.'

Mary and the 'Gardener'
(*John* 20: 15)

One of the most poignant stories in the whole Bible is that in which Mary Magadelene, on the first Easter morning, failed to recognise her risen Lord.

It was very early and Mary had gone along to the tomb of Jesus in the company of some of the other women in the group. Their intention was to complete those customary embalming procedures which, on the Friday afternoon, they had been able to attend to only in a hasty and partial fashion, owing to the imminent approach of sunset. For sunset brought the beginning of the sabbath, since the Jewish day ran from sunset to sunset (approximately 6 pm to 6 pm). During the hours of the sabbath no tasks such as embalming or burial were permissible.

Jesus's body was delivered for burial only when dusk, and thus the sabbath, were very close at hand. As a result there had not been time to carry out the embalming as it was normally done and as they wanted to do it. That was why the women came very early to the burial place on what we now know as the first Easter morning.

When they arrived at the tomb they found it empty. In perplexity and some fear they scattered. Mary ran to tell the disciples of their strange finding. Peter and John hurried to the grave to see for themselves and, when they had confirmed that it was really empty, went their own ways. Mary was naturally not able to run so fast as they, and moreover she was exhausted by her dash to tell them what she and the others had discovered. She, therefore, followed some considerable distance behind so that, by the time she reached the tomb again, the men had already been and gone.

When Mary looked in on the grave she saw two men there who asked her why she was weeping. Her reply, that it was because Jesus was gone and she did not know where he had been taken, contained a wealth of sadness in its words. It was with a breaking heart and eyes misted with tears that she turned away. As she turned she caught a glimpse of someone standing near who also asked her why she was weeping. She imagined this figure to be the gardener and asked him, if he knew, to tell her where the body was.

Jesus spoke just one word. It was her name. 'Mary', he said quietly. At once she knew who he was and life for her was immediately transformed.

This is a beautiful story and a deeply moving one. It also confronts us with this most intriguing question: 'Why did Mary fail to recognise Jesus to begin with?' Several answers have been suggested.

Perhaps it was because *her eyes were so full of tears* that she could not see him properly. What a terrible blow it was to her when Jesus was crucified. Mary owed everything worthwhile in her life to him. He had plucked her out of the very gutter of life and made her a new woman. The result had been that she loved him more than life itself; and now he was dead. It was as if the sky had fallen in and she was utterly broken-hearted. All weekend she had been in the depths of grief and now even his dead body was gone.

It was no wonder that the tears came. She simply could not keep them back. They cascaded down her cheeks and, of course, they blinded her so much that for the time being she could not see anything with any clarity, certainly not the person standing close by. In fact she could barely glimpse his outline through her tears before she turned away from him to hide her embarrassment; and she assumed him to be the gardener.

Mary had lost a loved one and her tears of sorrow prevented her from recognising that, in spite of all, that loved one was alive. Sometimes it may be like that with us. When bereavement strikes us and a loved one dies, our eyes may be so filled with tears that we cannot see beyond our sorrow, and we fail to perceive that he is really still alive. Yet the fact is that, if he is in Christ's keeping, he has an even more glorious life now than he ever had before.

In one of his poems Rupert Brooke wrote these lines:

> War knows no power. Safe shall be my going
> Secretly armed against all death's endeavour:
> Safe though all safety's lost: safe where men fall:
> And, if these poor limbs die, safest of all.

Perhaps it was because she was *looking in the wrong direction*. Mary had turned away from Jesus. She had her back to him because she did not for a moment imagine that there was anything this unknown man could do to help her in her need. Yet the fact was that nothing could have helped her more and nothing did help her more once she turned to face the right way.

Sometimes we, too, in our times of deepest need, may look in the wrong directions for help and healing, comfort and strength. We turn our back on Jesus and drink feverishly of the broken cisterns of other things. We try this 'ism' or that philosophy, we try pleasure, we try work, we try all sorts of things to give us the peace, the courage, the resolution, the satisfaction that we crave. We try practically everything except the Jesus who alone can meet our deepest needs.

An artist once painted a picture which summed this up. The picture depicts a travelling charlatan standing in a village square offering his quack potions for sale. He is represented as holding out to the villagers a bottle containing the elixir of life, claiming that, if they will buy and drink, life will be transformed for them. The people press round him with hands outstretched, eager to sample his wares. The poignancy – and the point – of the picture lies in the fact that the charlatan salesman has taken up his stance right in front of the village cross. Its open arms extend their life-giving invitation to all and sundry, but no one is paying it the slightest attention.

No matter what validity there might be in these first two answers, there is no doubt that the main reason for Mary's failure to recognise Jesus in the garden was simply her *ignorance of the resurrection.*

She just did not know that her Lord was risen and so, of course, she had not the slightest expectation of seeing him there. This was the main reason for her remaining blind to his presence for so long.

Most frequently this is the chief reason today for people remaining blind to the presence of Jesus, despite their great need of the help that he could give them. They are simply not aware that he is truly alive and really present. And I am thinking not just of those who disbelieve the resurrection of Jesus but even more of those who do not disbelieve it but have no real awareness of it.

W M Macgregor, sometime principal of Trinity College, Glasgow, recounts how a young woman came round to see her minister after morning service one Easter Day in Fife, Scotland. Her face was shining as she said to him, 'I simply had to tell you. I've never doubted the truth of the resurrection of Jesus but today for the first time it came home to me that it was really true. And what a difference it makes.'

What a difference it makes to anyone and to everyone who becomes aware that Jesus lives. It enables him to face all things not only with a shining face, but with a shining heart, too. For the companionship of the living Lord renders him invincible in face of everything that life may bring and in face even of death when it comes.